TALKING POETICS FROM NAROPA INSTITUTE

ANNALS OF THE
JACK KEROUAC SCHOOL
OF DISEMBODIED POETICS

Talking Poetics from Naropa Institute

Edited by Anne Waldman and Marilyn Webb

Introduction by Allen Ginsberg

SHAMBHALA
Boulder & London
1978

SHAMBHALA PUBLICATIONS, INC.
1123 Spruce Street
Boulder, Colorado 80302

ISBN: 0-394-73569-2
LCC: 77-90884

Distributed in the United States by Random House
and in Canada by Random House of Canada Ltd.
Distributed in the Commonwealth by Routledge & Kegan Paul Ltd.,
London and Henley-on-Thames.

LIBRARY OF CONGRESS CATALOGING IN PUBLICATION DATA

Main entry under title:

Talking Poetics from Naropa Institute.
Based on lectures given at the Jack Kerouac School of Disembodied Poetics at Naropa Institute, 1974-1977.
Bibliography: p.
1. Poetics—Addresses, essays, lectures. I. Waldman, Anne, 1945-
II. Webb, Marilyn. III. Naropa Institute.
IV. Jack Kerouac School of Disembodied Poetics.
PN1042.T27 808.1 77-90884
ISBN 0-394-73569-2 (v. 1) (Random House)

Printed in the United States.

Acknowledgements

The four parts of *Empty Words with Relevant Material,* by John Cage, have been previously published in four places: 1) in *Active Anthology,* edited by George Quasha (Fremont, Michigan: Sumac Press, 1974); 2) in *Interstate 2,* edited by Carl D. Clark and Loris Essary (Austin, Texas: 1974); 3) in *big deal 3,* edited by Barbara Baracks, 1975; and 4) in *WCH WAY,* edited by Jed Rasula (Dover, New Hampshire: 1975). Each appearance of the piece has an introduction.

"Empty Words: John Cage Talks Back," from *Loka: A Journal from Naropa Institute,* edited by Rick Fields. Copyright © 1975 by Nalanda Foundation/Naropa Institute. Reprinted by permission of Doubleday & Company, Inc.

The Content of History Will Be Poetry, by Ed Sanders, has been previously published in his book *Investigative Poetry* (San Francisco: City Lights, 1976), pp. 1-16. This work was reprinted by kind permission of the author.

A version of the talk *Poetry and Politics,* by Lewis MacAdams, was presented by the author at Bob Perelman's 1220 Folsoms "Loft-Talk" Series, on June 30, 1977, in San Francisco.

With kind permission of the publisher, Jerome Rothenberg, in his piece *Changing the Past, Changing the Present: A New Poetics,* has used excerpts from *The Cantos of Ezra Pound,* Ezra Pound (New York: New Directions, 1970). Copyright © 1940 Ezra Pound.

Permission to quote "12 Songs to Welcome the Society of the Mystic Animals," from *Shaking the Pumpkin,* edited by Jerome Rothenberg, granted by Doubleday & Company, Inc. Copyright © 1972 by Jerome Rothenberg.

TABLE OF CONTENTS

VOLUME ONE

VOLUME TWO

EDITORS' PREFACE

ALL OF THE essays in this book are based on lectures given at the Jack Kerouac School of Disembodied Poetics at Naropa Institute in Boulder, Colorado. The earliest of these talks was given in 1974, the year that Naropa Institute was founded, and the most recent, in the summer of 1977. On the whole, these lectures were delivered to Naropa students as part of ongoing classes or seminars. The talks were taped and then transcribed. Finally, they were edited, in consultation and collaboration with the poets. It was left to them to decide the extent to which they wished the wording and format of their original talk to be altered. Some poets decided to make extensive changes; many decided to leave their talks in almost their original form. One poet decided not to look at the edited transcript at all. The majority of these essays read in a style that is similar to the way they were spoken, retaining a direct relationship among mind, mouth, breath, and page.

We tried to select material that represented different and unusual perspectives on poetry and the practice of writing, and we looked for talks that would be informative to emerging poets and students of poetry. We also tried to include some pieces that provide insight into the motivations, inspiration, and past experience of poets, as these personal reflections are of immense value to young working writers. Necessarily this selective process required the omission of much valuable material. We expect that further volumes on poetics from Naropa Institute may follow in the future.

We would like to thank the following people for their help in compiling this book:

—Allen Ginsberg and Michael Brownstein, faculty and directors of the Jack Kerouac School of Disembodied Poetics at Naropa Institute, for considerable advice in preparing the final manuscript.

—Carolyn Rose King and Jane Ellman at Shambhala Publications, who contributed extensive help in editing.

—Vajradhatu Recordings, for taping all talks and generously helping with tape copying for transcriptions. Thanks to Suzanne Head, Bruce Wauchope, and Wendy Nelson.

—Bonnie Shulman, Marcie Vaughn Krichels, Jane Moscovitz, Chris Miller, Arlyn Ray, Lou Crago, Steven Low, Phoebe MacAdams, Kelly Mink, Wendy Leighton, Jane Ellman, Sagaree Sengupta, Barbara Stewart, Richard Elovich, Bob Rosenthal, Betty Londergan, Susan Keith Noel, Jill Schumacher, and Bret Rohmer for transcribing and typing.

—Carlton Spiller and Michael Scholnick, who helped edit Miguel Algarin's piece; James Grauerholz, who edited William Burroughs' piece; and Paul Portugés, for Allen Ginsberg's essay.

Our thanks to Naropa Institute for providing support, help, xeroxing, typing paper, stamps, and clarity. Special thanks to Chögyam Trungpa, Rinpoche, the founder of Naropa Institute, and to Jeremy Hayward, Bill McKeever, and Mary Smith of the Institute.

Also a personal note of appreciation to Bruce Wauchope, Jennifer Webb, and Reed Bye, for giving over-all help and being there to pitch in or just listen when things got hectic.

Anne Waldman and Marilyn Webb
May 1978
BOULDER, COLORADO

INTRODUCTION

HEREIN FIND A selection of lectures from the Jack Kerouac School of Disembodied Poetics at Naropa Institute, Boulder, Colorado, over the years 1974-1977. Some poets talk about themselves, their theories, minds, politics, sources, methods, praxis, tell secrets of their art, reveal confusions personal and metaphysic, clarify edolons and say "Wow!" The situation of both poetry and criticism here is largely auditory—a reliance on oral transmission. Spontaneous methods both occidental and oriental are herein emphasized in the context of an American poetics which has moved from page to voice in the last century. The poets involved are not types who ordinarily would be called academic, many of them having achieved their mature work or notoriety under conditions far from academic comfort—that is to say all the teachers are inventive active poets rather than learned scholars observing others of the art; though as may be seen, all poets are scholars of their own praxis. A common characteristic of all these poets is attention to mind, mouth and page and the relations between each for the mindfulness that goes back and forth between page and thought. Chance operation so characteristic of post-Einsteinian world is included in this exposition particularly in the work of John Cage, Jackson Mac Low and Clark Coolidge. Though at first the selection of poets and their works may seem specialized, such display of variety of method is rare in any single volume of composition covering modern poetry. We have had the opportunity to include for the most part spontaneously mouthed discourses by eminent representatives of quite different historical tendencies, geographies & modes—from Robert Duncan's exquisite scholarly weave to Ted Berrigan's practical tips to young poets. Half decade after the breakthru compilation of *New American Poetics* by Donald Allen & Warren Tallman, here we have ripe discourses & transmissions by older poets who have survived their experimental youth as well as bright annals by young dynamiters newly arrived to poetry mind.

The book provides an advanced survey of the poetic history and theory of the last several post World War decades notorious for radical change in prosodaic means and classical reference of learning that opened new consciousness so widely advertised in the poetic arts of the American mid-Century and beyond—a survey pronounced by those very makers who've created a poetic revolution in their nation that spread to many fields: politics & visual arts, accompanied by new music, hairstyle and dress. This art revolution evolved into a liaison, if not marriage, with some of the greater classical traditions of the Orient—Hindu, Japanese and Tibetan Buddhist esthetics and meditation practice. This meeting place between east and west in Poetics is more significant than political conventions or mechanical automotive & petrochemical multinational convocations because Poetics itself is the original, primary social manifestation of mind. High talk.

We wish readers well in perusing these pages, many may have happy and agreeable times discovering the delights & intimate thoughts of William Burroughs & Robert Duncan; the methodic wordplay of Michael McClure, Ed Dorn & Ron Padgett; Philip Whalen's, Lewis MacAdams', & Diane di Prima's classic reading; Anne Waldman's personal encyclopedia; oral values of Jerome Rothenberg, Miguel Algarin & Ed Sanders; ideas of ancient mindbending in Michael Brownstein's head; my own rationalization of visionary experience as ordinary mind. I hope that younger students mystified by history, ignorant of the revolutions of the Word thru recent decade generations, will be able to find their own intuitive logics represented in this latest wave of common sense theory & exquisite analysis done live, by live poets. Initial impulse of Bodhisattvic generosity—poets talking to whatever students who would assemble for their teachings given frankly in classes specialized with meditators & poets—may be a unique quality in this book of "criticism." The motive was communication. The space was open for question & amplification. The circumstance was intimate, accompanied by private meetings, parties, encounters of old friends among the artists, makings of new friends among the generations, peripatetic amity, erotic community, meditative centering & balance. What may come of this community is for future annals & teachings to discover. Whatever the fate of the Jack Kerouac School of Disembodied Poetics, some climactic event has taken place in American poetry which will leave its imprint of frankness & wisdom on future American lyric thought. Traces of bohemian anarchism mixed with traces of elegant tantra, traces of Whitmanic inspiration and traces of rock-'n'-roll high sound are here combined in a spectrum of poetics rarely before observed in any nation. Poetry always had spiritual aspiration and at the same time was a practical observance of day-to-day language; we may find in these XX Century utterances the insight of much classic contemplation and the beginning of some historic synthesis. We thank the sangha of poets students transcribers typists listeners administrators patrons gurus & janitors who helped transmit these annals to print without consideration of reward.

Allen Ginsberg
Co-Director, The Jack Kerouac
School of Disembodied Poetics,
NAROPA INSTITUTE
August 13, 1977

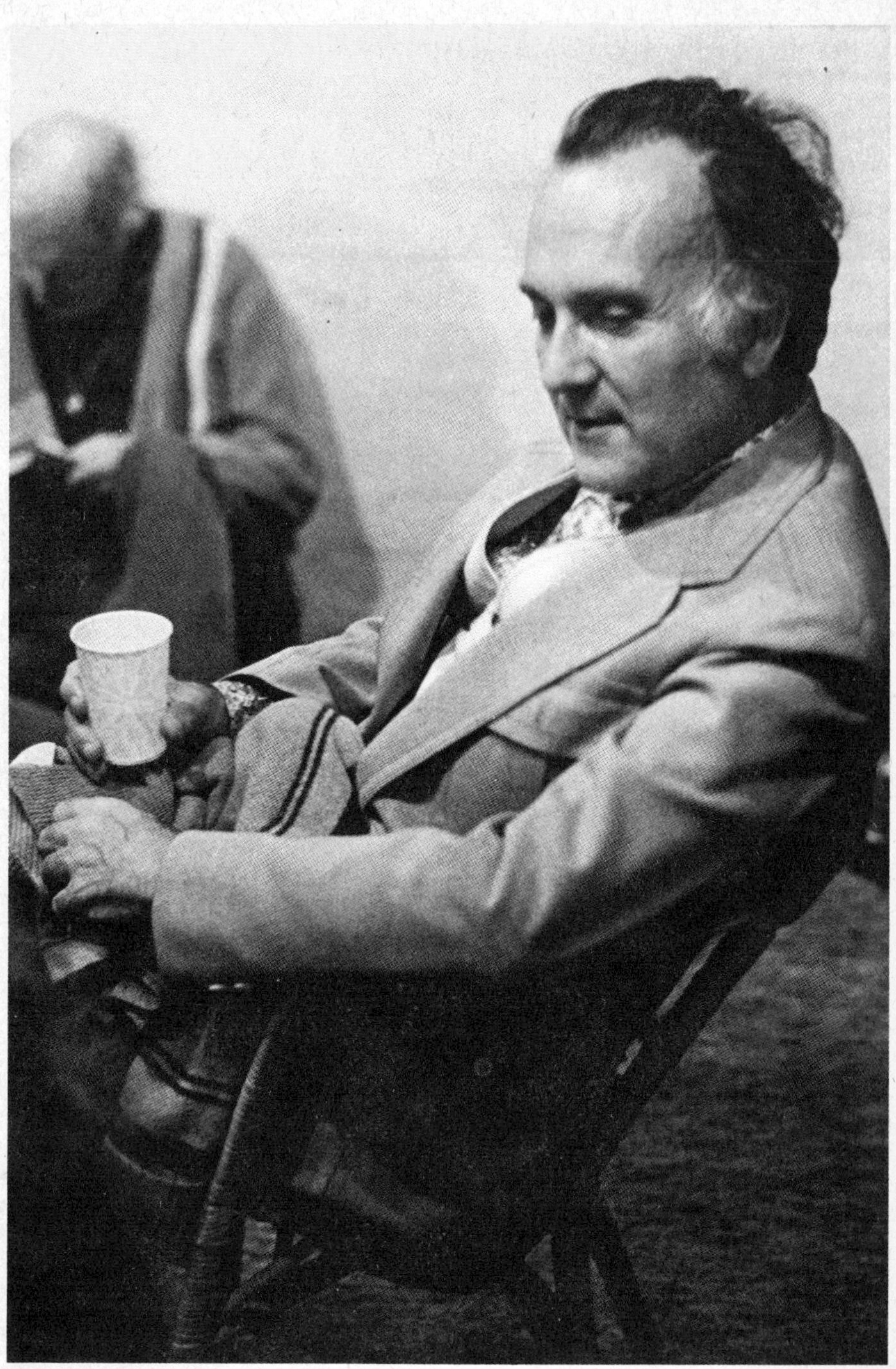

Photo by Andrea Craig

Robert Duncan

WARP AND WOOF: NOTES FROM A TALK

JUNE 10, 1976

STATEMENT OF THE "AUTHOR":

The following transcript of passages from a talk given at the Naropa Institute, June 10, 1976, has neither been read nor, it must follow, edited in any sense by me. I dislike intensely the idea of the publication of talk, which I would so distinguish on the one hand from a prepared lecture, and on the other hand, from writing. I am a writer, and as a writer, neither in poetry nor in prose, do I proceed without care and design. It must be made clear that while I was invited and paid to give a reading at the Institute, the lecture to the Institute was a free talk and I talked freely, rambling, and, as I remember—it is this that made for my not reading what I had said—frequently enough fishing and baiting various Buddhist prejudices I thought to be likely in my audience.

—Robert Duncan
San Francisco, March, 1978

I'M GOING TO imagine you all as utterly sublime, as Blake imagined, and also utterly stupid, so that I have a little room. I want you to draw a picture of what you think a section of cloth looks like with its warp and woof and have that before you—any of us can imagine this, can't we? We're sheer amateurs and we're just beginning to realize that we can make a kind of warp and woof and so we can see how things are crossing and undercrossing and crossing over. And then let's think about the fact that such a fabric, if gone into, may very well be seen to exist not just in two dimensions, as we see one side of the cloth, but we can see both sides of the cloth and also see its extension going through an entire universe.

One of the earliest ideas that comes flowing forward into the art world is that there is a true universe there, and those of us who are addicted to fabrication believe that the entire universe is truly a fabric, made-up, and that we are consequently in tune with it. So you see, when we think about poetry we've got a very wide picture, because we include much more in poetry now that mankind is coming in to the totality of its inheritance, more so than the word poetry originally proposed at all.

I will give you an example of a juxtaposition that came very quickly. The word "poetry" is a Greek word for making something up. It means to create; it means to make up. And so when you say, is that true, or did you make it up, you're really saying, is that true or is it poetry. And the idea that there was the possibility of poetry, or a song, doesn't mean that you made it up, does it? Much of the time when I am writing I think, "Oh, come off it, I'm really just sounding off on the bough of a tree like a bird does and whatever comes into it comes into it, but I'm just singing." Poetry is a very strange and possibly local idea.

The Jewish community, the entire Semitic community, which of course would include the Moslem world, felt very assaulted indeed when this, to them, decadent Greek idea of a made-up world came about. Think of the psalms, which are songs, and think of the voice that's present in the Old Testament, or the voice that's present in the Moslem world and in the inspired voice of Mohammed, as against the many inspired voices in Greece. If you were inspired, according to Jewish and Moslem law, if the spirit came and spoke through you, one thing you would not ever do with that would be to make it up. You were supposed to have it flow straight, not interfere with it. And so in the period of the thirteenth century in the Jewish community, and earlier in the Talmud, they interpreted the prohibition in the Old Testament to mean that within the cult of Yahweh you should not make a graven image. If you were going to keep that cult, that was part of your contract, your vow. And they saw that it also meant that you should not make a poem. You should speak with a voice coming from your heart, from your breath, that would flow into the divine breath and heart, and it would flow forth and you would never interfere with it.

In its extreme, of course, it was the prophetic, vatic voice of the poet. And so when I describe a poem, it is full of highly contradictory elements. I want you to remember that for myself, I am solidly a spirit of that conjunction of the Jewish and the Celtic world and the category that I didn't explain yet: the great idea which came down from Greece, that of making a poem, of fabricating.

In the Greek religion, at the same time, the idea of fabricating a poem, which included both making a poem and lyrics, became singing. Singing continued and it was thought of as a personal voice, not a made-up voice, but I think you can see that poets also made-up the very persons we hear singing. Within the Christian world, which is very strongly, of course, Judaic, there was a strong sense that there was something profoundly wrong about making-up persons. God was the creator and you were stepping into the Creator's place. So there is no drama within the Christian world until you come to the very period when Christendom thoroughly fell apart, and you find pouring forth from the Renaissance the making-up of persons. That creational God then had entered and gone entirely under the realm of the imagination.

In his withdrawal from the stage in *The Tempest,* Shakespeare made elaborate statements about a state of grace within himself that the audience extends to him. It's charged in every way with the earlier grace that within Christendom has been thought of as the devout relation to the universe. Shakespeare had announced that the universe was a stage and Shakespeare, of course, is a master-maker.

Not only did the Greeks have the term "maker"—Poet—but so did the Germanic-Celtic world. Our word "maker" is identical with the word "poet," and Chaucer and Dunbar, both referred to themselves as makers, not singers. And so, let's go back to that picture of a fabric. Storytellers must have thought of themselves as makers; they made the story up and they talked about weaving a tale. And it may be that telling stories, being able to weave a tale, not just telling what happened, but being able to weave a tale, goes along with being able to weave cloth. And the beginnings may very well have—their very core may have been the story you told as you wove the cloth, as the cloth was being woven.

A tale is amazing. We are lost in the maze, we strive to go to the center of the maze, we strive to return from the maze. The story of the poet-weaver belongs to the story of fabrications and is out of place in other constructs.

I think that all of the psychoanalytic world is now entering the imagination and again can be part of this fabric. But you can see the pretension of the poetry that I join myself to. It's much more ancient than this psychoanalysis; it goes all the way back to Homer, where he has a picture of a woman at one end weaving the tale that he is weaving himself, and a woman at the other end weaving the tale. At one end you have Penelope who is everything, and she's working away on a vast design which very well may be the design of the plot that her poor husband has to go through before he can get back to her.

The idea of the poet is to make the plot as cunning as you can; weave the weaving so you feel you know the warp and woof throughout and you've got the whole thing plotted. You're weaving in and out—one thread goes under, the other thread goes above. Out of this is the business of weaving whole areas of designs generating themselves throughout the endless spinning of cloth. And I'm also talking about a Hellenistic idea that the world was such a fabric and that weaving, in its first discovery, was not just a craft. I mean it's playing so that the warp and the woof are double events throughout this whole structure.

Our period of mankind has come to know that it is one species, and it's been a very recent trip indeed. Our present little cult of ecology thinks they're living wrong in New York, but Aborigines, on a day when they can't really find their grub, feel they're living wrong there too: we're so coming together that the fabric throughout is beginning to be consubstantial. And it's poets who announce very early that that fabric is consubstantial. And one of the great poets—and his greatness in my inheritance is that he *saw* and he is the person most disturbed by our coming to recognize that life is consubstantial—is Pound. He said that all events in history are contemporaneous. But he added that all human spirit is identical and our true identity is, as a matter of fact, human. We begin to see that if you were to name yourself human, you were an enemy of life, and if you were to name yourself living, all life ravens upon the universe, and so you would be an enemy of the universe. I mean, there is not a living form that isn't working away day and night to demolish the earth it lives on, chew, chew, chomp, chomp, scrabble, scrabble, dig holes in it, the whole thing. In this fabric, where are you going to put yourself? And yet the great adventure is to even have an identity in the species. Pound, with this "all kinds are contemporaneous" then identified the image in a different way than Plato had proposed, before the Greeks even thought about it. All men see things, and I'm now talking about a seeing that in this seeing will flood throughout your life, but that's anything you see, as a matter of fact. Plato talked about it—he proposes that ideas are ideas of ideas and that ideas are over there. But the great trouble was, what do you see when you see inside your head? What do you see?

Now let's think about present—a present given you, but also the present, the moment right where we are. The idea will be present and will be in the presence of the idea, or the poet's presence—this was the great term Pound had, one term he had and it worked for presentation not expression:

we don't squeeze it out of ourselves, we evoke a presence and presentation. We're in a fabric of time and space. The imagination is trying to imagine, and the great imagination addresses itself, as you do to a figure, to the presence of this fabric or what's going on on the earth, and in that, it has full force.

I have absolute faith that I am doing something; that I am actually sort of giving a picture here of where I am. I have faith throughout with everything, *everything*. That everything is going on and that's the piano I play. I love the *little* piano where you can understand the whole thing: they can explain it to you octave by octave—man, that learning has been so tampered with, that you don't even have to listen, you can do it by the numbers on the piano. It's a tampered scale, it's one lovely invention, like our powerhouse, it's a very local one, and in full confidence you could hear a discord and you could also hear it didn't belong to the music. No, I'm going to the *big* piano of that vast fabric and I run up and down that fabric like your friendly local spider, cheering little flies to turn into poetry spiders. "Come on fly, I don't want to eat you; I've eaten too many flies. Why don't you spin some little webs. I mean, don't you catch on? Here you are wrapped around the whole thing. How fly, how come you are whining and buzzing and carrying on, that's not a song you should. . . ." But then if you come into the web and say, "I want to do a web"—I think probably everyone of the foolish flies, those flies that come into poetry, continuously are always coming on like they're tough. "Did you notice my web?" says the fly. He didn't notice that the web was just spun around him and that he is really drying up a bit and will be a leftover inside one of those awful webs we spin. That's a warning to you all: don't pay attention to the webs of the poets. If I impress you, especially don't pay attention; if I don't impress you, you're in for free, but if you're going to go into poetry, don't pretend you're not a spider.

Let me give you a hint of where you don't have to be if you don't get involved in poetry. If you're not going to be a story weaver, a weaver of stories; if you're not going to be making-up and creating things, you could gloriously be back in the Song of Psalms singing inspired out of your human spirit, like a bird does, singing to the air floating around. You could also be like the bard in the Celtic world, keeping alive, in its eternal recitation, the identity of a tribe. But you could also be a bard.

Bardically, I keep alive the identity of the universe, which is our great tribal story. Our science today is sitting where all the lunatics sat before and told the Sioux that they were Sioux—got it down real straight so that the one little group of Semites could know that they were different from all the rest of those awful Semites and certainly different from those other people. All of those tribal things, all of us Celts, were carrying on keeping a happy island, a happy Scotland going forever. Our great tribal thing today is to tell us about the universe we live in, to perpetuate our identity, which is where our great myth today is—it is written by our physicists and chemists who are imagining the universe. They aren't imagining our tribe. And *that* I find fascinating, because it, too, comes in and feeds poet-lore. Luckily, that picture changes all of the time. Maybe those tribal pictures did too. I'm sure tribes didn't want to live in the utter dullness of being the same all of the time.

One thing they found out, when they went to Indian tribes in California, is that there were tribes who made up whole new identities for themselves year in and year out—made up new languages, made up new stories about where they came from. Anthropologists had wanted to think that tribes kept stories for hundreds of thousands of years with no creative activity at all. I mean they never changed then, nothing, they were the same people, because they met these people living in these strange ways and said, "Man, that must be the way they lived before they learned how to live. That must be way before the Bible, I can see that. It don't even look like the Bible, it must be, gee, leftover from some other age."

And then you can read anthropologists in the thirties who

are still worried about, "Isn't this a stone-age man?" Is that more impressive than the cannon man or the atom-bomb man? And that is so recent—I couldn't invent an atom-bomb so I must be. . . . As a matter of fact I couldn't invent a rifle, so what am I? Actually, I find out that, food-wise, I'm a food gatherer, mushrooms, berries. Everything else seems too energetic for me, so no wonder I want to put away this picture of primitives. I am the confusion that exists. Food-gatherers don't want to keep things straight. If a food-gatherer has a map he's already eaten up everything on the territory he is going to. So, a food-gatherer has to go out there with no map, man, or he's never going to stumble on a new group of mushrooms, not at all. If you gather things, the last thing you do in the world is to take a hikers' map and go along and try to find some food; that's covered territory. So, actually, in poetry, I write that way too. We're back at that fabric. So let's say one more little thing about this fabric.

Today we have people reviving the crafts, and so we find fabrics made again and with quite a marvelous range of what can happen in those fabrics. This Duncan, he makes rugs. None of them are complete. There are sometimes imaginary parts of the same rug, which is enormous. It's very practical, but enormous when you start making it. They're hooked rugs and, of course, I think you can guess that I do not have any pre-plan, so I simply have designs moving out of designs, moving out of designs, and then I lapse from them and leave them. As a spider I'd look like—they did some experiments on LSD spiders, they lose track of the web, they can't make it all of the way through. They can see it before they do it, and then they get bored and walk away. Eventually, of course, in my imaginary world of art, there would be enough time that anybody coming along, an archeologist for example, could see that this belongs to a design somewhere.

As a matter of fact, we know that now about ourselves. Most great clues we've got are only fragments. A little tippy-toe mark of a dinosaur and they can draw the whole dinosaur. We leave imprints wherever we go, and a design. Design, the content, the things that we first respond to in a poem and think are tremendous, I think are to be read as imprints. And how we design, devise the design which flows as we work—one level convinces us that we devise it as we find ourselves imprinted throughout the thing. We can't not be. A poet searches for his voice. The place that makes sense is to go out and get the voice from some crazy thing, pick it out of a hat or go to a dream or something else: that's where the voice is.

When I was growing up the thing that was in schools, they wanted you to write with your true voice and not come on like you were Robert Browning, which I wanted to come on like. I was Robert Browning, and then I wanted to be a whole series of things. Well, actually, it did begin to dawn on me that when I come on like I am Robert Browning, one thing I'm not is Robert Browning, and I don't get to be anybody but me, so that question is so simple—imprint that is. And yet, that's what's alright when there are masses of poetry, masses of poems to read: read them.

If I center in on the individual poem, I can imagine its occasion, but if I have to do that, it means that the poet has not created its occasion and I have to imagine it. And most people who ask you, what do you think of this, are really saying, will you think about this for me? That's their first step and actually all of us, when we have our little critical responses and come in and want to tell somebody about a poem, should remember that we're actually telling ourselves something about how we hear it and how we read it: how we get it. That's where we got our critical insight. And the strangest thing about reading is that it is the same intuition we know writing is, clearly. If you read the poem at all, however you hear it, you have had to create it. Those words were sitting there in the same sense that they were—if I write a poem it's not an idea coming out of me—it is an idea in those words. No matter what I have inside of me, and no matter what I think I have said in that poem, the words say what they say because they are a shared storehouse of human experience. This is our fabric, the language is, and it's very specific. It's really like a warp and a woof. Take its meanings: you can't give meaning to a poem. Impossible. And it is literally impossible for any personal individual experience to enter language at all. It can't find itself there, but what it can find is its common human experience.

Language tells us that we are individuals, but that's not our idea. One thing that could dawn on you is that you're discovering yourself in a commonality when you're in words and emotions. The idea that there is an archetype, either deep in your psyche or in a metaphysical world, is nothing compared with the fact that *language* is flooded with archetypes as we write or read. Powerhouses and residence these words are, and they're built into a vast fabric and they extend way back in time.

Photo by Ellen Pearlman

Diane di Prima

LIGHT/AND KEATS

JUNE 24, 1975

IT SEEMS TO me more and more as I get more and more deeply into poetry that the actual stuff that poetry is made out of is light. There are poems where the light actually comes *through* the page, the same way that it comes through the canvas in certain Flemish paintings, so that you're not seeing light reflected *off* the painting, but light that comes *through,* and I don't know the tricks that make this happen. But I know they're there and you can really tell when it's happening and when it's not. So I've been trying to figure out what makes it happen. And I think it's not very different from the light of meditation. So that I'm beginning to suspect that what makes it happen is *the way sound moves in you,* moving your spirit in a certain way to produce a certain effect which is like an effect of light.

And I want to read you something about the way sound moves in you, the way the sound moves in the hearer. It's from the second book of *Natural and Occult Philosophy* by Cornelius Agrippa, which was written in the 1400's. In the second volume of this three volume work, Agrippa gets a lot into numbers. When he gets into numbers, he gets into music. When he gets into music, he gets at one point into the fact that vocal music is the most effective of all musics for moving the hearer. And what he has to say about vocal music is not that very different from the effects of a well-read, well-chanted poem:

> Singing can do more than the sound of an Instrument, inasmuch as it, arising by an Harmonial consent from the conceit of the mind, and imperious affection of the fantasy and heart, easily penetrateth by motion, with the refracted and well-tempered Air, the aerious spirit of the hearer, which is the bond of soul and body, and transferring the affection and mind of the Singer with it, It moveth the affection of the hearer by his affection, and the hearer's fantasy by his fantasy, and mind by his mind, and striketh the mind, and striketh the heart, and pierceth even to the inwards of the soul, and by little and little, infuseth even dispositions; moreover it moveth and stoppeth the members and the humors of the body. . . .

He goes on to say that breath is, of course, spirit, and that what happens is the spirit, your spirit as a person singing or chanting or reading the poem aloud, enters the ear and mingles in the body of the hearer, with his spirit, and so moves and changes the body's humors and dispositions. What we are is nothing but a physical instrument, not much different from a musical instrument in some ways, and the effect that we produce—or perceive—of light or any other really high energy—meditative high—comes only out of changes in this physical instrument.

And so, there is a way, to me, that the most high aim of poetry is to create that sense of light. There are passages in the *Cantos* that do that. There are poems in every language that do it, and it's a question of some real subtle juxtapositions of vowels. Pound tried to track it down when he talked about the tone leading of vowels and harmonizing the different vowels, and Duncan is into that when he talks about assonance and "rhyme." Like picking up the same vowel over and over for a long time and then changing it.

Or paced—spaced—repetition of sound. Pound tried earlier to get at it when he wrote—in his critical essays—that we've always in recent centuries had a *stressed* beat in English verse, whereas the older quantitative verse, where some syllables are more drawn out than others, gives more the sense of music. It also gives more the space for that phenomenon of light to occur.

One thing that I have just a glimmer, have a handle on, that I really think maybe is worth thinking about, is this phenomenon of light, in all, maybe in all arts. *How it could suddenly burst into light in your body,* if it does.

Another, not really separate thing that I wanted to do today is to share some passages of the letters of John Keats with you. Passages about the writing of poetry. They were maybe my earliest information on what poetry was about. Just like the most recent information I have is this of the breath and the light, for me the earliest information was this that I want to read you next. When I was a youngster I had been reading a lot of Western philosophy and novels and came upon in a book, a novel by Somerset Maugham, a quotation from Keats. And then I pursued finding Keats and discovered there was poetry and wondered why anybody did it with philosophy, when they could do it in a poem. And you can do it different in a poem every day, you can make a different construct. You can make a different reality every day instead of sticking to your system for the rest of your life, like poor Schopenhauer. So, at that point I fell totally completely passionately endlessly eternally in love with John Keats: And mainly the information that was in his letters.

Keats was born in 1795 and died in 1821 at the age of twenty-six. These letters were written between 1817 and 1820, so Keats is in his early twenties: twenty-three, twenty-four, like that. This first quote just gives you some sense of his sense of commitment to poetry:

> *April 17, 1817.* I find I cannot exist without Poetry—without eternal Poetry—half the day will not do—the

> whole of it—I began with a little, but habit has made me a Leviathan. I had become all in a Tremble from not having written anything of late—the Sonnet overleaf did me good. I slept the better last night for it—this Morning, however, I am nearly as bad again.

Less than a month later, he begins to really get into it—get led by the pursuit:

> *May 10, 1817.* I've asked myself so often why I should be a poet more than other men, seeing how great a thing it is—how great things are to be gained by it, what a thing to be in the mouth of Fame—that at last the idea has grown . . . monstrously beyond my seeming power of attainment. . . . Yet 'tis a disgrace to fail, even in a huge attempt; and at this moment I drive the thought from me. . . . However, I must think that difficulties nerve the Spirit of a Man—they make our Prime Objects a Refuge as well as a Passion . . . the looking upon the Sun, the Moon, the Stars, the Earth and its contents, as materials to form greater things—that is to say ethereal things . . .

At this point, he's climbing in some sense, *out,* really climbing out of the matter universe, and there's a flicker, kind of a flicker of a real gnostic consciousness: how we have to climb back through all the realms, all the concentric spheres of matter, like the planetary spheres, the zodiacal spheres, back into the immaterial. And one way to do that—use it all up. Every minute.

Let's go on. Here's a quote about the long poem.

> *October 8, 1817.* —why endeavor after a long Poem? To which I should answer, Do not the Lovers of Poetry like to have a little Region to wander in, where they may pick and choose, and in which the images are so numerous that many are forgotten and found new in a second Reading: which may be food for a Week's stroll

> in the Summer? . . . Besides, a long poem is a test of invention, which I take to be the Polar star of Poetry, as Fancy is the Sails—and Imagination the rudder.

I find myself very often when I'm reading something that somebody gives me, I find myself saying, you sound like you're just getting started. You know, at the point where the poem finishes. Why not go on for twenty, fifty more pages? 'Cause what we tend to like to do is kind of put our toe in?—or like peek in through the door but stay on the threshold. And if you go past the point where you know what you're talking about and then thru all the blather that comes after that, you *might* come out in an inner chamber, you know? You just might. You might blather for the rest of your life—a lot of us do—but that's a chance you gotta take. Anyway . . .

Here's a take he did on genius—a take on what a "man of genius" is.

> *November 22, 1817.* —Men of Genius are great as certain ethereal Chemicals operating on the Mass of neutral intellect—but they have not any individuality, any determined Character—I would call the top and head of those who have a proper self Men of Power . . . I am certain of nothing but of the holiness of the Heart's affections, and the truth of Imagination. What the Imagination seizes as Beauty must be truth—whether it existed before or not,—for I have the same idea of all our passions as of Love: they are all, in their sublime, creative of essential Beauty. . . . The Imagination may be compared to Adam's dream,—he awoke and found it truth:—I am more zealous in this affair, because I have never yet been able to perceive how anything can be known for truth by consecutive reasoning—and yet it must be. Can it be that even the greatest Philosopher ever arrived at his Goal without putting aside numerous objections? However it may be, O for a life of Sensations rather than of Thoughts! . . . I

> scarcely remember counting upon any Happiness—I look not for it if it be not in the present hour,—nothing startles me beyond the moment. The Setting Sun will always set me to rights, or if a Sparrow come before my Window, I take part in its existence and pick about the gravel.

This quote has for me three different nuggets. First, the thing he goes back to later and often about having—here he says the man of genius and later he says the poetic character—having no individuality. Later, he goes into it in more detail and talks about partaking in the life of every creature. Really, what he's trying to get at, or describe, seems to be some kind of real egoless state. There wasn't that vocabulary in England, thank God, in 1817—thank God because otherwise he might have said, "Hey man, I just reached a far out egoless state the other day, watching this sparrow," and we wouldn't have what we've got.

Then, Keats' idea of the imagination, which is really not that different from Blake's. *The imagination creates worlds.* It brings into being whatever it can vividly and completely conceive. "The imagination may be compared to Adam's dream, he awoke and found it truth." Creative imagination: that idea keeps growing with him all through his life. Somebody, a little old lady in Phoenix—it was one of those question and answer periods after a reading—asked me what I thought the function of the poet was in this society. And I said that if you could imagine anything clearly enough, and tell it precisely enough, that you could bring it about. Anyway, the theory of imagination as creative principle keeps growing for Keats. It is for him—as for Blake—a cornerstone.

And the third thing here—for me, one of the guiding sentences of twenty years of my life, or maybe still, maybe always—is, "I am certain of nothing but the holiness of the heart's affections and the truth of the imagination." That about says it.

OK, this next is a paragraph that really got Olson off, he quotes it a lot—it's the passage on negative capability. It's very interesting and these things: imagination, genius as a kind of egolessness, are all part of it. There is a system here, if you wanted to systematize it, there is a growing system of thought that Keats is evolving, but systematizing it would be simplistic—it would do him an injustice. As he said, "I have never yet been able to perceive how anything can be known for truth by consecutive reasoning." I want to just take the quotes and look at them—follow him chronologically through the process.

> *December 22, 1817.* -[*The winter solstice, by the way.*] The excellence of every art is its intensity, capable of making all disagreeables evaporate from their being in close relationship with Beauty and Truth . . . several things dove-tailed in my mind, and at once it struck me what quality went to form a Man of Achievement, especially in Literature, and which Shakespeare possessed so enormously—I mean *Negative Capability,* that is, when a man is capable of being in uncertainties, mysteries, doubts, without any irritable reaching after fact and reason. Coleridge, for instance, would let go by a fine isolated verisimilitude caught from the Penetralium of mystery, from being incapable of remaining content with half-knowledge. This pursued through volumes would perhaps take us no further than this, that with a great poet the sense of Beauty overcomes every other consideration, or rather obliterates all consideration.

So, at this point what he's calling a sense of beauty, what obliterates all consideration or all thinking process, is that same experience that we have *whenever* it all drops away. A kind of satori. My friend Katagiri Roshi, who's a Zen master in Minneapolis, gave six lextures once on the word WOW. WOW, as the complete American Zen experience. When it all drops away, when the sense of beauty obliterates all consideration, or the sense of the overwhelmingness of it. Wow, that's all we said for the last three days, me and my two friends, as we drove here from California, through all this incredible country, and we kept saying. . . . They were asleep one night and I'm driving, and saying Wow, Wow.

Negative capability. Now you see how that idea, first of the man of genius not partaking of any individual character, becomes a bigger or more universal idea, which is that idea of negative capability, of *not pursuing any viewpoint*. It's kind of a real Eastern idea. Except that it happened fresh from nothing at this point in this kid in some dumpy English suburb. "When a man is capable of being in uncertainties, mysteries, doubts, without any irritable reaching after fact and reason." And to get that state, clearly enough focused to make it the matter of poetry, so that you don't try to "make sense," but become this receiving tube, become this focusing point.

QUESTION: Your statement that the role of an artist is to see clearly and precisely—

DIANE DI PRIMA: I didn't say that was *the* role of the artist. I had been asked, how does the artist function in society? I'm not saying that the high role of the artist is to function in society at *all*. But the way that your art does function socially is that when you can visualize clearly any possible human state, or social state for that matter, or universe, and focus it clearly and precisely enough, and then bring it into being either verbally in a poem, or in a painting—you bring that world into existence. And it's permanently here, it doesn't go away. Doesn't even go away when the book gets burned, look at Sappho. Those worlds don't go away.

Q: Do you see any contradiction between that and a statement by Picasso that one should have an idea of what one wants, but not too precise an idea.

D.DP.: Oh no, I don't see any contradiction. Because, you see, the idea of what you *want*, it's just your launching pad, just what you start off from, it has nothing to do with what you make. When you get through that threshold and you enter the chamber, *that's* where you start to see clearly. If your idea is too precise, you might be at that door forever. You know, 'cause you might have the wrong combination for the lock. For example, I might say I know this next part of this poem has to have that feeling of line that they had in paintings in Sienna. I don't mean I'm going to write about the paintings of Sienna. I don't mean anything but that I have a *feel* of something about to happen there. That's a non-precise idea, and at that point, that's all you have. And then when you enter into the act of composing, at that point you have nothing—everything drops away, and you have only what you're receiving. Your whole purpose as an artist is to make yourself a fine enough organism to most precisely receive, and most precisely transmit. And at that point—total attention to total detail, total suspension of everything but that vision, whatever it is, and again, at that point, no idea at all, no idea. The idea was just your first—the idea is what made you get up that morning and put your shoes on. And when you find yourself in an incredible grove, it's not because you had an idea you were gonna get there. But when you get to the grove, you damn well better open your eyes. It's two different parts of the process.—More Keats?

> *February 3, 1818.* Poetry should be great and unobtrusive, a thing which enters into one's soul and does not startle it or amaze it with itself—but with its subject . . . we need not be teased with grandeur and merit when we can have them uncontaminated and unobtrusive.

I remember a lecture by Shunryu Suzuki where he said that the essence of great art was monotony and loneliness. "Uncontaminated and unobtrusive."—Should I be saying more?

Q: How do you understand "unobtrusive"?

D.DP.: I keep coming back to landscape, though actually it's anywhere, it's in music, it's everywhere: there's a place where the most absolutely amazing things that exist in the material world are also the most natural, and you say "Of course!" Your whole being says of course. It's unobtrusive in the sense that it doesn't—there's no jagged edge—it doesn't have to stick out in any way. Uncontaminated in that you're not talking *about*, you're presenting a thing. It's there. You needn't be teased by it. A pretty picture of a great landscape is a tease. The landscape itself is unobtrusive. It enters you, you enter it, it's there. The same with the great recreation of landscape in painting—it's not trying to be landscape. It's simply itself. Uncontaminated. A new order of reality. And just there. Unobtrusive.

Because finally art isn't *about*: there's no idea and there's even no symbols, there's the thing you've made.

> *February 27, 1818.* 1st. I think poetry should surprise by a fine excess, and not by singularity; It should strike the reader as a working of his own highest thoughts, and appear almost a remembrance.

When you see that land, or you recognize that feeling, you say, yeah, wow, I remember this, I've been here before, even though you never have. The most surprising things are always familiar, immediately. That's been my experience. They're immediately familiar, they're from another realm, we're now living in still—all the time—we just don't pay enough attention.

> 2nd. Its touches of beauty should never be half-way, thereby making the reader breathless, instead of content. The rise, the progress, the setting of Imagery should, like the sun, come natural to him, shine over him, and set soberly, although in magnificence, leaving him in the luxury of twilight. But it is easier to think what poetry should be, than to write it—And this leads me to Another axiom—That if poetry comes not as naturally as the leaves to a tree, it had better not come at all.

Three things, three "rules" or principles, in this particular letter. First: "Poetry should surprise by a fine excess and not by singularity." Unobtrusive. Dig how he qualifies that—

excess, but *fine* excess. Second, "Its touches of beauty should never be halfway, thereby making the reader breathless instead of content. "The rise, the progress, the setting of Imagery"—look how this almost is a description of a process that can occur in meditation—that did occur for Keats, I'm sure, in the *composition* of the poem, and that he proposes the poem itself should recreate in the reader—"The rise, the progress, the setting of Imagery should, like the sun, come natural to him, shine over him, and set soberly, although in magnificence, leaving him in the luxury of twilight." And third: "That if poetry come not as naturally as the leaves to a tree, it had better not come at all," which I would like to sort of send as a telegram to every literary magazine and English department in America.

> *April 8, 1818.* [*A little description.*] The innumerable compositions and decompositions which take place between the intellect and its thousand materials before it arrives at that trembling, delicate and snail-horn perception of beauty.

The insistence again on the light touch, a really fine (not sharp) edge: negative capability. Fine excess. "Trembling, delicate and snail-horn perception of beauty."

> *May 3, 1818.* An extensive knowledge is needful to thinking people—it takes away the heat and fever; and helps, by widening speculation, to ease the Burden of the Mystery. . . . The difference of high Sensations with and without knowledge appears to me this: the latter case we are falling continually ten thousand fathoms deep and being blown up again, without wings, and with all the horror of a bare-shouldered Creature—in the former case, our shoulders are fledged, and we go through the same air and space without fear.

The way he talks about knowledge there is almost a Buddhist sense of knowledge. Without knowledge high sensations give us just that sense of falling, and there's no way to simply allow it, allow them to occur. Unless you can allow what Keats calls Sensation with that negative capability, you'll never get out of where you were in the first place, never pierce the veils. A Buddhist statement, really, or a gnostic one—in the full sense of gnosis: knowledge eases the Burden of the Mystery.

> *October 9, 1818.* Poetry must work out its own salvation in a man: It cannot be matured by law and precept, but by sensation and watchfulness in itself—That which is creative must create itself—

"That which is creative must create itself." This is an attempt to describe the workings of the creative imagination—that thing which spins itself out of itself. Experienced also in meditation. "Sensation and *watchfulness.*" I think you can see here that poetry was for Keats—can be for us—a complete practice, a form of what Suzuki Roshi called "Way-seeking Mind," leading us to knowledge. The creative creates itself.

> *October 27, 1818.* As to the poetical Character itself (I mean that sort, of which, if I am anything, I am a member; that sort distinguished from the Wordsworthian, or egotistical Sublime; which is a thing per se and stands alone), it is not itself—it has no self—It is everything and nothing—It has no character—it enjoys light and shade; it lives in gusto, be it foul or fair, high or low, rich or poor, mean or elevated—It has as much delight in conceiving an Iago as an Imogen. What shocks the virtuous philosopher delights the chameleon poet. . . . A poet is the most unpoetical of anything in existence, because he has no Identity—he is continually informing and filling some other body. The Sun,—the Moon,—the Sea, and men and women, who are creatures of impulse, are poetical, and have about them an unchangeable attribute; the poet has none, no identity—he is certainly the most unpoetical of all God's

> creatures. . . . It is a wretched thing to confess; but it is a very fact, that not one word I ever utter can be taken for granted as an opinion growing out of my identical Nature—how can it, when I have no Nature? When I am in a room with people, if I ever am free from speculating on creations of my own brain, then not myself goes home to myself, but the identity of every one in the room begins to press upon me, so that I am in a very little time annihilated—not only among men; it would be the same in a nursery of Children . . .

This is, I believe, where he most insistently tries to come to terms with *having no Nature.* The open space in which the poem occurs. That theme, "not myself goes home to myself," you know, but the identity of every creature . . . harks back to that earlier passage I read about the man of genius having no individual character, as opposed to what Keats calls "the egotistical Sublime." Only now—a year later—he much more urgently tries to get in there and explore, talk about, that open space. Maybe it would have been better if Buddhism *had* come to England, because he would have had some mechanisms for dealing with that loss of self. He might have had techniques for being that man of genius and remaining centered, so that maybe he wouldn't have gotten sick. You get sick when you can't handle any more energy, right? It's interesting that in the same letter I was just reading he goes on to say, "I will assay to reach to as high a summit in poetry *as the nerve bestowed upon me will suffer.*"

Amazing that these are just letters to people: his brother, his friends. Astonishing letter to get in the mail. "Oh God, another letter from Keats, I'll read it later. Can't make head or tail of anything he says. Why doesn't he just tell me how he's *doing*?" [*Laughs.*]

> *March 19, 1819.* The greater part of Men make their way with the same instinctiveness, the same unwandering eye from their purposes, the same animal eagerness as the Hawk. The Hawk wants a Mate, so does the

> Man—look at them both, they set about it and procure one in the same manner. They want both a nest and they both set about one in the same manner—they get their food in the same manner. The noble animal Man for his amusement smokes his pipe—the Hawk balances about the Clouds—that is the only difference of their leisures. I go among the Fields and catch a glimpse of a Stoat or a fieldmouse peeping out of the withered grass—the creature hath a purpose, and its eyes are bright with it. I go amongst the buildings of a city and I see a Man hurrying along—to what? The Creature has a purpose and his eyes are bright with it. But then, as Wordsworth says "we have all one human heart"—There is an electric fire in human nature tending to purify—so that among these human creatures there is continually some birth of new heroism.

Whew! [*Rereads line.*]: "There is an electric fire in human nature tending to purify, so that among these human creatures there is continually some birth of a new heroism." Way-seeking Mind, again. As, indeed, "We have all one human heart" speaks of the universal Buddha-nature, doesn't it? It goes on:

> The pity is, that we must wonder at it, as we should at finding a pearl in rubbish . . . I am, however young, writing at random, straining at particles of light in the midst of a great darkness . . .

This light—of which Body is the ground—do you see how Keats insists on our physicality? "The noble animal Man" is something Michael McClure might come up with, as in the preface to *Dark Brown,* he says, "to get in deeper touch with our walls of meat." This light, of which in the open space of poetry or meditation, Body is the ground—*is* the light that comes through the poem, and, with enough skill, is *created* (or evoked—drawn forth) in the reader *by* the poem.

> *September 24, 1819.* The only means of strengthening one's intellect is to make up one's mind about nothing—to let the mind be a thoroughfare for all thoughts—not a select party.

Constantly harping on that openness, that negative capability, that letting it come *through* you. Leaving behind opinion and judgment—the first requirement for tuning the instrument in poetry, and in meditation.

The last thing he had to say about the writing of poetry, in a letter to another writer (August, 1820) was: "You should load every rift of your subject with ore." And the last thing he had to say altogether, about himself as poet, was in his last letter. It was written to Charles Brown, his friend and sometime roommate, in England:

> If I should die tomorrow, I have left no immortal works behind me, nothing to make my friends proud of my memory. But I have loved the Principle of Beauty in all things, and if I lived, I would have made myself remembered.

He stayed that clear. His sense of humor stayed with him, too. The last line of that same letter is "I cannot tell you goodbye, even in a letter. I always made an awkward bow."

Q: How important is the knowledge of other poets—chronology and all that business—how much do you have to know to write poetry?

D.DP.: Depends on how long you have to live, I guess. Look, the more you read and fill up your head with cadences, with rhythms and vowel patterns of other poets, the more of a repertory you have to draw on, conscious and unconscious, when you're writing. A lot of what you do is variations on riffs you've already heard. In this sense, poetry, like jazz, is a kind of dialogue that extends through time.

Of course, poetry has to come out of *you*—but there's the work on the "you." The more you've refined the instrument, the more gradations of tonality you program into it, the more information—history, myth, biology—you program into it, and the more you increase your capacity for carrying energy—literally carrying current—then the more you'll have available when the poem seeks to move through you. More range, subtlety, power—"understanding" in the non-thinking Zen sense of "understanding." You can lend yourself to the poem with a wider range of possibility.

Q: How come the Romantics—how come everybody draws on them? How come the Romantics happened?

D.DP.: It's interesting that you say now we draw on them. When I went to school, it was considered very gauche, very contemptible to be involved in reading any of the Romantics. People read T.S. Eliot. Now you say we draw on them, that's news to me, I'm glad to hear it. I grew up in a world where this was what you *didn't* talk about: this whole body of stuff was too lush, too emotional, and not intellectual enough. You'd be more likely to read Dryden. Anyway, aside from that, your question is—How come they *happened.*

This Romantic movement is not an isolated thing, it didn't just suddenly happen. It was a thread, a way of seeing and feeling, all through the so-called Classical period. A kind of steady, esoteric current. The Romantics were always there.

Q: Would you say the Romantics differ from Classical artists because of more heart space, as opposed to intellectual space?

D.DP.: I don't know that there can be more heart in the world than there is in certain Classical people: Schütz, Buxtehude, Palestrina. Shakespeare—would you call him Classical? [*inaudible*] Well, Dryden is full of heart. I don't know that there's more heart space. There's a different mode, a different emotional tongue. It's played in a different key. I can't say more or less feeling. It's obvious to me that the Romantics thought a lot, too, as much as anybody else. So I mean you can't say heart/intellect, you can say a different quality of motion, a different tone. A modality of light.

Actually to me, if you think of the Romantics, you've got

to think of a certain way of conducting your life, or taking control of your life, which at that point was desperately necessary; because the first Industrial Revolution had already occurred, England was rapidly becoming the ugly empire. They were at the same point, in a lot of ways, that we were at during the fifties. Maybe. So that what you have is you have this incredible burst of heart energy against the mechanization of human society, whether it's Shelley, or Blake. You know, that's a good point—are you going to call Blake a Romantic, or not? What are you going to call Christopher Smart?

Q: How much are you influenced by your readings of Gnosticism? How much have you taken into your work?

D.DP.: Basically, there is the belief, in most forms of Gnosticism, that the spirit stood somewhere outside of this matter universe, and had fallen into it. That the universe itself was a trap. A cage that had trapped particles of spirit, and the point to the various kinds of meditation and mantra—spells—that they practiced, they had very complex spiritual disciplines, was to learn how to release the spirit from matter, and send it home. Out of the matter universe. This is kind of simplistic, but more or less true of most forms of Gnositicism, I think.

To me there is a whole progression in Western thought, and it starts with—hell, it starts with the stars, it starts with where did the people come from that made Sumeria, Mohenjo-Daro, Egypt. Isis says she comes from Sirius. OK, let's forget about that. Let's play with modern Western thought, and start around pre-Classical times, where you have almost a kind of Taoism, a sense that the universe is basically good, fertility is good, the natural sexual rhythm is good, and most of the ritual celebrations, at least the exoteric ones, have to do with keeping those cycles. Fitting yourself into the grain of the wood, and being joyous about it. Though, probably the mystery cults taught even then that *this is not our home*, the material world is only a disguise to penetrate, an alphabet to read, to get at the true kernel of things. Still, the basic feeling is one of *accord*. OK.

Gnosticism comes in off the wall—probably out of the Middle East—and makes a big thing out of this-is-not-our-home. Blows it up into No, this whole thing is a hideous monstrosity, it's a prison, a trap, the only thing we can do here is get out of here as fast as we can. If we could remember for one minute who we really are, we couldn't possibly stand all this blather of the four seasons and fucking and vegetation cycles and moon cycles and all, we gotta get *out*! OUT! Like that.

OK, so then it's there and it's a real strong religious movement. For a long time it's larger and more influential than Christianity. Christianity to my mind sits on the fence. The universe? It's real and it isn't, it's good and it's bad. From around the fifth century A.D. on, anyway, Christianity has been nothing but a tool of the state—whatever state. When the Roman Empire couldn't continue working in its old form as empire, it co-opted Christianity and continued to be the Roman Empire, under guise of church, and marched clear across this continent to the Pacific Ocean building roads and making laws, and is now marching across Asia. It's the same Roman Empire. However, that's neither here nor there, because that's not a line of thought, that's a march of the ants or something like that.

Anyway, to get back to this other progression. So the Gnostics are there, and they're saying no, we gotta get out of here. There are many incredible, beautiful, epic-type scriptural poems and allegories where you have your image form, or ideal self, whatever, out there in the spirit world and he-she comes and wakes you and reminds you who you really are and you begin making the slow progress back out of the concentric spheres. As you fall in, as this piece of spirit falls into the matter world, it passes all the planes and finally it passes through the planetary spheres. And each one of them is guarded by a daimon, or archon, who gives you an attribute or aspect of your personality. Your true spirit doesn't have all this personality. You fall through, and Saturn gives you one load of garbage and Jupiter gives you another, and finally you get here and you're surrounded by all these sheaths of matter. A lot of Gnosticism spent a lot of time studying scriptures they had similar to the Book of the Dead—practices by which as you left, you dropped off the characteristics of each sphere, so you could arrive in the empyrean—or past it—pure.

I'm giving a really simplistic view of the whole thing. There was no orthodoxy in Gnosticism, there were as many beliefs and groups as sprang up, and they each lasted as long as they lasted, and became as influential as they became. In one system, there are the pure forms of energy—or whatever, inexpressible—and then the forms after that, that became the creators of the matter universe, and why these fell and decided to become creators, which was an ego trip. And in one case (one myth), Spirit is tricked by nature. Nature falls in love with Spirit, and she becomes a smooth pool of water and reflects his image and he falls in love with his own image and falls into the pool, which is nature, in order to embrace himself, and that's how Spirit is trapped in matter in one story. There are so many. There's a dragon under the sea guarding the pearl, and the pearl is knowledge of who we truly are and how to go home. Many, many metaphors.

According to the history books, Gnosticism was wiped out by 500 A.D.—one more piece of bullshit that we've been taught, like Europe being a "continent." If Gnosticism was ever wiped out, it was much later; it was in the Age of Enlightenment. The so-called Age of Enlightenment, when we forgot almost everything we ever knew in Europe. What happened till then was it went underground and kept changing its forms and every time a heresy surfaces, a so-called Christian heresy surfaces in Europe, it has some of these same characteristics. The largest movement, the Albigensians or the Cathars in southern France were in many respects a revival of the old Gnostic religion. But it came up again and again: in eastern Europe, in Muenster as the Anabaptists, in the Brotherhood of the Free Spirit that Hieronymus Bosch belonged to, in the early Rosicrucians, in William Blake—over and over everywhere and it's still in the European blood and head.

However, a big step forward was made—I think that we're working out a whole series of problems as a whole race, probably every race in every galaxy has its things it's working out, and we're working on this particular one—and the next step in working it out happened at the point when people began to get a glimmer that maybe, just maybe, spirit is trapped in matter for a reason . . . ? More than just to climb out again. That maybe there's a way to take the whole thing with us. To truly transform the matter universe. And at this point, alchemy becomes a serious business. It deals with the question, which is still the question, the real millenial question: *how to make paradise on earth.* How to transform the matter universe so that the spirit, which has fallen into matter finally, like yeast in bread, fills everything. And that's as I see it, as far as we've got in all that. That's the one we've been struggling with, as far as I can see, from around 1200 or 1300.

This is really a simplistic view of European thought, and I just give it to you for what it's worth, because it's been useful for me as a handle to hang stuff on, different bodies of work, different people's thought. I'm totally influenced by Gnosticism, if in it you include all those heresies, because I feel that that's my heritage. My tradition. That I come out of a Europe that's almost completely forgotten what it was, because the Church did such a good brainwashing job, but that was a place of strong shamanism, of medicine religions, out of which grew this Gnostic root. Which Gnosticism in turn fed and nourished. Every Christian heresy went back to some tribal form: resuscitated free love, held property in common. And at one point ten thousand people were drowned in the Rhine in one day—I mean it went on and on. And I feel that I'm an escapee. I feel that that particular tradition is my tradition, and that the information I have to receive comes through the study of these forms.

For instance, when I began to understand how completely the concept of alchemy—not making gold, simply—transforming lead to gold is only part of the process of transforming this samsara. Or it's a means of focusing mind. Both.

Making light. That's what it's about. Transmutation was a basic axiom in Europe for a thousand years, just like now the scientific method, or cause and effect, whatever, is the basic axiom of our culture. And once you clue into the fact that alchemy was not some speculation but the basic ground they took root in, the basic belief that their thought went out from, it changes what you hear when you hear the music, it changes what you see when you see the painting. And if you can really get your head into a place where you see the premises of alchemy as axiomatic—the law of correspondence, the transformation of the matter universe—then you start to clue into a lot of stuff. Anyway, in that sense I've been influenced.

Q: There's one thing from the letters—straining at light—seems to go back to what you were just saying.

D.DP.: "I am however young, writing at random, straining at particles of light in the midst of a great darkness . . ."

I have to say that the Gnostic position is very strong in Pound, very strong in Robert Duncan; it runs like a thread through the Romantics, and it's here, now. So, who was wiped out in 500 A.D.?

"Straining at particles of light in the midst of a great darkness"—that's Keats.

"In the gloom, the gold gathers the light against it"—that's Pound.

Q: I was just wondering about *Loba* and how it got started. It's a very complete work in many ways.

D.DP.: OK let's see. There was a point at which I had been home for a number of years, and living as I thought I should live—zazen, macrobiotics, all that—and at one point I suddenly got a job teaching poetry in Wyoming to schoolchildren, and found that Wyoming, the parts that I was exposed to, was filled with so much pain, so much no-touching, so much no-loving, so much anger and these kids were in such a hungry place—all the usual boring stuff like teachers paddling people and all that, and Indian kids with almost no shoes having to run track in the snow, and nearly everyone always drunk or drinking—but there it was, there was so much for me to absorb, plus, also, I had lived on the kind of food I believed in, all those years, and I found myself thrown into a world where there was nothing to eat but steak and liquor. And you know, I came home from this experience, which was only a two-week experience, and I was sick for a month. I hurt all over my body. Everything hurt. I went to my homeopathic doctor, who was eighty-eight years old, and he said: "Toxins! Toxins in all the cells! A toxic condition of the system!" So, I went to bed and hurt a lot, and ate little homeopathic pills, and had a lot of dreams that were replays of various really heavy incidents: a girl at the reform school taking me on a tour of the building and showing me the solitary cells for thirteen to eighteen year olds, the face of a gay watercolorist who commits himself over and over to the state madhouse—trip after trip. I just had all these dreams, and slowly as I integrated this information, it got clear that there was nobody to blame. There was nobody in Wyoming that you could point to and say, "There's the villain, let's kill him!" and then it would all be OK. *There was no villain.* There was just a situation of people living in total pain. And as I began to absorb that information into my system, the dreams changed, they stopped being replays of classrooms and so on, and they got more and more symbolic. And finally, I had a very long dream one night. I won't go into all the parts of it, it had to do with having to find shelter somewhere, being in an outcast or vagabond situation with two of my children, and living in the cellar of this building in which some very rich people lived upstairs. They were getting ready to have one of their entertainments: they were going to watch through kind of skylight-things in the floor, while we were hunted down by a wolf. I found this out by going upstairs and spying on them, listening to the conversation. I decided I wasn't going to wait to be hunted. I picked up my baby, and had another kid following behind me, and I was with a friend whose baby was really noisy, and I was worried about the noise because I was afraid it was going to give us away, and we started to walk through this incredible stone labyrinth. As we were getting it together to go, down the ladder that

I'd used to spy came two men with a wolf between them, trussed as if she had been killed in a hunt—you know, legs tied to a long piece of wood. When they got the wolf downstairs they untied it, and it's the wolf that's supposed to hunt us. We were already walking out. We weren't running—we were walking out. And this wolf digs that this is what's happening, and falls in behind us and starts walking with us. Keeping pace. And at some point, I turned around and looked this creature in the eye, and I recognized, in my dream, I recognized or remembered this huge white wolf, beautiful white head, recognized this as a goddess that I'd known in Europe a long long time ago. Never having read about any European wolf-goddesses, I just recognized this as deity. We stood and looked at each other for a long moment.

And then we emerged later—there's another part to the dream, which is interesting in terms of Wyoming. We emerged into the sunlight and all these rich folk were doing a dance in the rain, a circle dance with magical gestures. And the children without any question ran and joined the circle. I joined in, too, and then I began to wake up, and my head said—wait a minute, you can't join these folks, they're the bad guys. They're the bad guys and they're making all this pain and suffering, and you cannot dance this dance with them. And I was half awake and half asleep, and falling back asleep, and the voice of this friend of mine who'd been dead eight years at that point, said to me in his usual tone, annoyance and exasperation, Fred Herko said to me, "Di Prima, if you go on thinking like that, you're going to be sick for the rest of your life." And I woke up.

OK. I didn't start writing *Loba* then. The dream was a dream. I always write down my dreams. I wrote it down. A year later I was teaching in a classroom again, this time in Watsonville High School. There's barbed wire around the playing field, guards all over the place—an absolutely horrible situation full of the kids of the migrant farm workers. Out of the blue, I had to drop back and let the other poet continue the class alone, because there were some lines being spoken in my ear, and they had to be written down or they wouldn't go away. That happens to me sometimes.

They turned out later to be the first lines of *Loba,* although at that point they didn't make any sense, I didn't know what they were about at all. "if he did not come apart in her hands, he fell / like flint on her ribs . . ." Who's writing that, I didn't know. The next day the process happened again, and when it happened a third time, those first three little sections, it began to zonk back in, not to that whole dream, but just to that vision of that wolf head, with the white ring about it. And then, two years later, in Part Four of *Loba,* I finally got the dream down. It's the first time I ever consciously turned a dream into a poem, although dreams turn into poems all the time. Let me read that part to you. It's called

DREAM: THE LOBA REVEALS HERSELF.

she came
to hunt me down; carried down-ladder trussed
like game herself. And then set free
the hunted turning hunter. She came

thru stone labyrinths worn by her steps, came
to the awesome thunder & drum of her
Name, the LOBA MANTRA, echoing
thru the flat, flagstone walls
        the footprints
                footsteps of the Loba
                        the Loba
drumming. She came to hunt, but I did not
stay to be hunted. Instead
wd be gone again. silent
children in tow.

she came, she followed, she did not
pursue.
        But walked, patient behind me like some
big, rangy dog. She came to hunt, she strode
        over that worn stone floor
tailgating, only a step or two
                        behind me.

I turned to confront
to face
Her:
ring of fur, setting off
the purity of her head.
she-who-was-to-have-devoured me
stood, strong patient
recognizably
goddess.
Protectress.
great mystic beast of European forest.
green warrior woman, towering.
kind watchdog I could
leave the children with.
Mother & sister.
Myself.

I have one little thought I want to throw in and then we can stop, and that's that we're all sitting or meditating or studying or whatevering in one form or another—this thing I was saying about the progression of European thought, the working out of a problem, whatever. Paganism, Gnosticism, alchemy and then what—where do we go. Way-seeking Mind, "that which is creative must create itself." I want to say that the old religion and the old forms that we're all studying with such total devoutness—Eastern and Western—they have a lot of information and they have a lot of the means, but where we're all going they haven't mapped yet. We're mapping it now—or it's mapping us. If Buddha really had done it, we wouldn't be here.

Sources

AGRIPPA, CORNELIUS, *The Natural and Occult Philosophy.* Written in the 1400's, translated in 1667 into English. 3 vols. To be reprinted soon by Samuel Weiser of New York.

DI PRIMA, DIANE, *Loba* (Berkeley: Wingbow Press, 1978).

KEATS, JOHN, *Complete Poetical Works and Letters of John Keats* (Cambridge: Houghton Mifflin, 1899).

Photo by Cynthia MacAdams

Ted Berrigan

THE BUSINESS OF WRITING POETRY

JULY 9, 1976

As ALL OF YOU presumably know, Allen Ginsberg's father passed out of this life, and Allen went back to New Jersey. This was to be Allen's last class this term, and part of it was planned to be about Philip Whalen, who will be teaching this class next term. However, since most of you here were at my own previous class, in which I talked about the business of being a poet, in this class I want to talk about the business of poetry itself. I'll let Philip introduce himself to you when he arrives next week. Something, incidentally, that he can do very well.

In New York City in the early sixties I recall many times hearing the poet Frank O'Hara, who was an important figure to me, say of something that he liked very much, that it was very amusing, and say of things that he didn't like very much, well, that wasn't very amusing, was it? And that's come to me to be a sort of criteria for works of art in general. That is, those that are not very amusing are usually not very amusing because they are not any good. All the works that are good are amusing. The problem with saying this in a classroom is that one tends to think that amusing means funny. Amusing doesn't mean funny, necessarily. It means, if you take the meaning of the word strictly, it means something like that it turns you on. That it turns your muses on. That it makes you respond to it. Your muses respond to its muses: while you're responding to it, the response is going on on many levels. It is amusing to read a poem like *Kaddish,* for example, which is about a rather gruesome subject matter. It's amusing in that it's beautiful, it's wonderful, it's gorgeous, it's touching. It's also horrifying, it's scary, it's vulgar. It's shocking. It's all those things, all those things have to do with being amusing. I wish I could think of a parallel example to say what is not amusing, but I'm not really interested very much in things that are not amusing. It would not be so amusing I suppose to read a poem for example that was a haiku and said, "Allen Ginsberg's father died yesterday and I felt sad." It's amusing to think that someone might write that down and that would be a poem. It's almost amusing enough to be a good poem, but it's not *quite* amusing enough. Maybe it is amusing enough. It all depends on whether the poem is by a good poet or not. Now that's another poem.

I'll tell you a story, actually, which you may know already. The Argentine writer Borgés tells a story about a man whose ambition in life was to write *Don Quixote.* What was that guy's name? Pierre Menard. And his ambition was to write *Don Quixote.* And *Don Quixote* had already been written. See. So there was a difficulty there. Not an insurmountable difficulty perhaps, but a difficulty. So he thought that what he would do would be to live . . . if I don't get the details of this right, if I get some details wrong, and you know better, don't correct me, please—I mean it's how I'm telling it that's important, not the story, I mean, for the purposes of this class. Pierre Menard thought that first the best thing that he could do in order to write Don Quixote would be to live the life of Cervantes. Now Cervantes was born in a certain place, so you know he couldn't really do that, but there were other things he could do. Cervantes had lived in a certain part of the world, he had been a soldier, he had been in prison, he had been on voyages across the seas and so on. Now this guy thought he would do all of these things. He would live as much of Cervantes' life as possible, literally all of Cervantes' life except for actual birth and babyhood, and then he would of course be able to write *Don Quixote.*

But, of course, he soon realized, as one must realize it, that that would take too long. He didn't really have 40 years to spare, or 50 years to spare, to get ready to write *Don Quixote.* He wanted to write it right now. So, and there's more to that, but the point is that he then decided that he would not do all that, he would simply write *Don Quixote.* Just sit down and write it. So, he wrote *Don Quixote.* Well, he wrote at least the first twenty pages. He may have written the whole thing. But, he wrote *Don Quixote,* and Cervantes wrote *Don Quixote.* And if I remember correctly, the rest of the story by Borgés consists of a word by word comparison & analysis to these two *Don Quixote*s. And now, they are exactly the same. The exact same words. Because they both wrote *Don Quixote.* But the point is, & Borgés makes this clear in the critical analysis of the two *Don Quixote*s, that while the two books contain exactly the same story, in the same words, that Pierre Menard's *Don Quixote* is vastly superior to Cervantes' *Don Quixote,* when one realizes how difficult it was to write *Don Quixote* after the telephone, the airplane, trains, & electricity had come into being. As opposed to how much easier it had been to write *Don Quixote* before the existence of these things. It is a point well taken. But it's not a very interesting point, otherwise. What's more interesting is that Pierre Menard did write *Don Quixote.*

Larry Fagin, when he teaches class, likes to give out work-sheets with poems on them that don't have the authors' names after the poems. Poems by the famous dead & the famous and moderately famous living. And then you get to talk about the poems, you being all of you. And then—but there is a secret in there. Because *Larry* knows who wrote them, because he selected the poems and typed them out. And so he's got you, in a funny way. And—but he's brilliant enough to think that he really hasn't, that that doesn't really give him any edge. Because he has an idea, which is that the poem is more important than the poet. But the poem is not more important than the poet. Not one bit, actually. Not as long as anyone *knows* the name of the poet.

What I'm suggesting here, is that you take out about three of your best poems and think who your favorite poet is, living poet preferably, and type that poet's name in underneath your poems, and then put them in the drawer for a few weeks, and then find them, and read them, and see if they are good poems by that poet or not very good poems by that poet. And it may give you some sense of where you are at. It's an interesting idea.

And Part Two of that is, I was thinking what I would do if I were a teacher and Allen Ginsberg were my student. And he came up to me and he said, "I've just written this longish poem called *Howl*, and he showed it to me, Parts I and II. And I took it home and read it. Now, I like to write poems about 14, 15 lines long. And so I would bring it back in the next day and say, "this is pretty good. Why don't you cut it down to about 14 lines?" I mean, that's likely what I *would* say, probably. You know, or maybe I would say, "why don't you break this up into about five sonnets?" Well, in the old days Allen probably would have done that, he really might have done it, I don't know. But, I mean, that's what Allen does to you people. And you must be aware of that. I mean that's what *any* teacher, particularly a poet, will do to you. They're trying to get you to be good poets, and they know what good poetry is, because they write good poems. So they're saying you should write poems the way they would write them. You especially should rewrite your poems the way they rewrite. Now, they're very clever these poets, and they *don't* want you to write poems that are *like* their poems. They just want you to write poems the *way* they would write them if they were writing your poems. Don't do it. Don't ever do it. I mean, except for when you're *imitating* other poets; then you *should* try to write like the poet you are imitating.

When you begin writing, you don't know *how* to write. Presumably most of you have already begun, but it's never too late to begin over. I mean it's necessary to begin over constantly. And the best thing to do when you begin is to pick some poet whose poems you like, and imitate some. And then find other poets & other poems and imitate them. The worst thing you can do is to tell anyone who you are imitating. Because then everyone will think that all the good parts in your poems come out of being a good imitation. When, in fact, the exact opposite will be true. The good parts will come out of where you misunderstand entirely what the poet you are imitating is doing, & so write something that is completely dumb, but that turns out to be very good. Misunderstanding is one of the truly creative procedures in writing.

In 1960 & 61 I wrote a bunch of poems saying "it's 5:15 a.m. in New York City & I'm doing this & that & now I think this & this & this, & next this happens, that happens, & in conclusion I can say blank blank & blank." I thought I was blatantly imitating Frank O'Hara. But I was wonderfully dumb, and thank god! It turns out that when Frank was writing his poem and saying it is 4:16 a.m. in New York City, he meant that it wasn't 4:16 a.m. at all. It was a flashback. Whereas when I wrote my poems, whatever time I said it was, that's what time it was. So, I wrote an entirely different kind of poem than he did, and not only that, but in the language of the critical periodicals, I actually extended a formal idea of his into another area, actually extended his formal idea into another place. And my poems were pretty good too. And in fact they're not very much like Frank's at all, because I was too dumb to be like Frank. But I wasn't too dumb to be like somebody. So I did that actually. All right. I want to read you a few poems that I think are amusing. The trouble with these two books is—I have two books that I'm going to read from. One is called *The New American Poetry*, edited by Donald Allen, this book is out of date, generally, it was also better than 50% crap when it came out anyway, and a lot of it was out of date already then, too. But there's enough in it that's really great, that you should want to have it anyway. There are poems in here that will just survive, you know, and that are really very good. But if you discover this book newly and freshly and read through it, you're liable to fall into the error of liking and imitating all the poets in here that are horrible. Don't do that. Now it's important when you write poems, to write good poems. Better yet, it's not so important to write good poems, because, that's what academics do; what it's important to do is write *terrific* poems. And there's no reason why you can't do that. All you have to do is look at lots of poems by poets that are terrific, whose poems are terrific, and see what makes up a terrific poem, and then write some terrific poems yourself. You'll have to use parts of the way that they did it, but you will think of some ways yourself. One way, for example, to write a terrific poem, is to have every line be terrific. As has been pointed out here I think, by some of the teachers, if you can't think of any terrific lines, just take them from other poets. I wrote a couple of poems by taking some translations of John Ashbery's and typing them up double-spaced, so that there was room between every line for another line, and then I wrote a line between every line, making my line run into his next line. So that I was literally interrupting him. And then I retyped them and left out all his lines, and then I tidied up what I had, and what I had wasn't very good, but I was able to take some of it and put it in some other poems, some of it did come out very good. What I'm saying is that there are a lot of ways to write terrific poems, but there's only one way essentially to write poems that are no good. And that's to be not very amusing. And so don't do that, don't be unamusing. Don't write poems about how much you love your dog. Unless you can make a terrific poem. On the other hand, don't write poems about the death of your father unless the death of your father and how you feel seems much more important than how terrific the poem is. The only way you can make that be is by having the poem be *so* terrific that it's not noticed. I want to read some poems, I want to read particularly a section of a poem. This is a part of Frank O'Hara's poem *Ode to Michael Goldberg ('s Birth and Other Births)*.—It's an ode. An ode is a great form. Because, there's no exact definition of what in the hell it is. It's a poem, with elevated subject matter written in elevated language. The best thing to do, if you want to write an ode, is to get a dictionary of poetry and poetics and look up and read all about what an ode is. The language of the definition is completely vague and general, but you'll be saturated by it with what an ode is *supposed* to be, and then you can start writing in this high falutin' way, that ordinarily you would think is very phony. But the fact is that there are many different ways that human beings talk, and while it's necessary to be able to write or sometimes write the way you talk all the time, it's also a very good thing to be able to write some of the time the way you don't get to talk too often. And sometimes to write in ways that you hardly ever get to talk, but that do correlate with ways that you do get to feel. Exaltation is a feeling whose language we don't ordinarily use in everyday life, but we may want to write about it. This is the final section of Frank's poem, called *Ode to Michael Goldberg ('s Birth and Other Births)*. And there's nothing in it about Michael Goldberg or his birth, it's all about Frank's birth and coming alive and having reached the age he is at the time. This is about the last 20 lines maybe.

I am assuming that everything is all right and difficult,
where hordes
of stars carry the burdens of the gentler animals like ourselves with wit and austerity beneath a hazardous settlement
which we understand because we made
and secretly admire
because it moves
yes! for always, for it is our way, to pass the teahouse and the ceremony
by and rather fall sobbing to the floor with joy and freezing
than to spill the kid upon the table and then thank the blood

for flowing
as it must throughout the miserable, clear and willful
life we love beneath the blue,
a fleece of pure intention sailing like

a pinto in a barque of slaves
who soon will turn upon their captors
lower anchor, found a city riding there
of poverty and sweetness paralleled
among the races without time,
and one alone will speak of being
born in pain
and he will be the wings of an extraordinary liberty
1958

Now that's pretty good, really. There's no reason why you can't write that well. This guy could do it, and he's just a guy, you know. I mean he was just a guy, he was born and brought up in Massachusetts, and he's just a little Irish guy who died younger than I am now. And there's no reason why you can't do it. I mean it was done in your time, in our time. He just had a thought that he would write some odes, and he wrote them because it was a scary idea, actually, because most odes that have survived in the English language, are great poems. Like *Ode to a Nightingale,* and so on. And Frank wrote nine odes, I think. And about six of them are really very good. And two of the other three are pretty good. And the other one is a joke. It's a deliberate joke. But it's funny. I want to read another poem that's amusing. If I can find it. Here it is. I'm sure that you've been read this. Nevertheless. . . . I use this form all the time myself. I first read this anthology, which is called, was called then, *The New American Poetry, 1945-60,* in 1959 which is amusing in itself, because, how could I read it in 1959 when it was poetry 1945-60? But it happened to come out in 1959. The editors just wanted it to have a great title. I mean, and they thought 1960 sounded better than 1959. And that's what happens in the world of poetry. And I remember when I read it I didn't know any of these, hardly any of these guys. I knew about a few of them. I didn't know much about them. I remember when I read this poem I suddenly understood everything about poetry. That is, at least I understood everything then. I don't, in fact I don't think I've ever understood any more than I understood then. But I didn't know what I understood. I couldn't really articulate it. But I understood everything. And so I had a long talk with Ron Padgett, who at the time was eighteen years old, and I told him everything I understood and then I didn't remember any more about it until a good number of years later, and then I asked Ron one time if he remembered that talk, and he said he remembered it very well, it had changed his life. So I asked him what I said, but he didn't remember either. But, in fact, since then I've had to teach this class in schools, teach this poem, and talk about it, and so those times when I had to talk about it I listened to what I was saying. And now I know what it is I understand. I'll pick up from there later after I read it. It's called, *Why I Am Not a Painter,* also by Frank O'Hara.

WHY I AM NOT A PAINTER

I am not a painter, I am a poet.
Why? I think I would rather be
a painter, but I am not. Well,

For instance, Mike Goldberg
is starting a painting. I drop in.
"Sit down and have a drink" he
says. I drink; we drink. I look
up. "You have SARDINES in it."
"Yes, it needed something there."
"Oh." I go and the days go by
and I drop in again. The painting
is going on, and I go, and the days
go by. I drop in. The painting is
finished. "Where's SARDINES?"
All that's left is just
letters. "It was too much," Mike says.

But me? One day I am thinking of
a color: orange. I write a line
about orange. Pretty soon it is a
whole page of words, not lines.
Then another page. There should be

so much more, not of orange, of
words, of how terrible orange is
and life. Days go by. It is even in
prose, I am a real poet. My poem
is finished and I haven't mentioned
orange yet. It's twelve poems, I call
it ORANGES. And one day in a gallery
I see Mike's painting, called SARDINES.

1956

Now there is one thing that you have to admit about that poem, and that is that it's amusing. In the fifties and on into the sixties, . . . these very poets, John Ashbery, Frank O'Hara, others were considered suspect by the great lords of poetry, because they were amusing themselves a good part of the time when they were writing. Which was definitely considered something that one was not to do when you were writing. Frank has a poem which begins, "At night chinamen jump/On Asia with a thump." It's in couplets. And ends: "We couple in the grace/Of that mysterious race." It's very beautiful, actually. As John Ashbery has pointed out, the editors of *Partisan Review* and magazines like that did not approve at all of such kinds of writing. But what is in *this* poem, what is Frank saying about why he is not a painter? That is, in every poem someone is speaking. Even in the poems you write. Even in the poems I write. If your name is at the bottom of the poem, presumably that's the name of the person speaking. Most of the time. Unless the poem is titled something like *The Love Song of J. Alfred Prufrock*. Then you can assume that it's J. Alfred Prufrock speaking. And not T. S. Eliot. Except at least at one removed. You assume, at least, that Eliot is arrogantly suggesting that he knows how to make a song for a different person than himself. No matter how much that person may be like himself. In every poem, someone is speaking. You tell from the poem what kind of person is speaking. That's how you get to know the person in the poem. That's the only way. You can possibly get to know from reading some other poems by that person. But those are about the only ways. You can't know more about John Ashbery's poems, or Anne Waldman's poems, by knowing those people personally. In fact you will most likely know less. If you saw Homer picking his nose, you might suddenly think that the Iliad is not that great, you know. But unfortunately the Iliad would still be that great, and you would be an nth degree stupider. Which would presumably change in time. But . . . the poem is entitled *Why I am not a Painter*. Why *is* that person who wrote that poem not a painter? as he describes himself in the poem. Does anyone know the poem at all? Come on, you people, I know that some of you *do* know it. I even know which ones know it, in some cases.

All right. How many think I should tell you?

QUESTION: Why don't you read the poem again?

TED BERRIGAN: I don't want to read the poem again, but I'd be happy to have you read it if you want to . . .

Q: I think he's saying that they're both doing the same thing, there.

T.B.: Well, they are both doing the same thing, he is saying that, they're both making art, and one is making it with paint. Which, incidentally, has some words in it. And the other is making it with words, which incidentally has something to do with color.

Q: And that each one, that the art or the work changes as it goes along, and the artist decides what to leave out?

T.B.: OK, I'll accept that, but how does that explain why the person writing the poem is not a painter, didn't get to be a painter?

Q: Well, he might have used that as a catch title, I really can't explain it.

T.B.: Yeah, OK, that is something I want to pick up on and that is, you don't use things as catch titles. You do use catch titles, but that's not the only reason why you use them. Good poets don't do that. John Ashbery told me once—I like to talk about John Ashbery, as you notice, I think he's a master poet of our time. I feel that gives me permission, because I feel that way about him, to talk about him anyway I want. But he told me one time that when he published his book *The Tennis Court Oath,* which made a big change in all our lives at the time it came out, that he had a problem in that he didn't have any poem by that title. *The Tennis Court Oath.* And he wanted to call the book by that title. So that he took the first poem in the book, which already had a title, I don't remember now what it was called, but it had a different title, and he changed its title to *The Tennis Court Oath,* and what he told me was that he was afraid it hadn't worked. And he didn't really elaborate. But one of the things that John Ashbery does quite consistently, quite often, is to come up with his titles before he writes his poems. He has been quoted, in fact, as saying that very often he needs a title to write a poem or else he won't know what he's going to be writing about. Or even how to write it. I get most of my titles after I do the poems. But I like titles, and I think it's very good to put a title on your poem. It's fun, and it can also be illuminating. You can call your poems, *#1,* 1975, or something, *#2, #3,* and so on, as some painters used to do. But—I always understood that poem of John Ashbery's in terms of what I know about its title: *The Tennis Court Oath.* And there is something that can be known about it. Do any of you know what the tennis court oath was?—It doesn't matter. But John Ashbery—that poem originally had a different title. But John changed it to that. Now, I've always thought the poem, finally called *The Tennis Court Oath* actually was something like a poem of Amy Lowell's called *Patterns. Patterns* could be called *The Tennis Court Oath* too, actually, and in a certain way it would be all right.

I'm suggesting a course of study, in a way; how you can look at the poetry of other people, poetry that is good poetry, keep in poetry that you think is terrific poetry. How you can study it in such a way that will be beneficial to you. The first and most important thing to have in mind is that you cannot figure out poetry. You can't as the saying goes in the colleges, "crack a poem." So that you know what it means and you don't have to give that a thought any more.

That's like getting married and thinking that you can crack your wife or your husband. I'm afraid that you may be able to do that, but you'll either get divorced, or you'll have another thought coming. You can't really know any more about a terrific person. You can know a lot of things about a poem, though. You approach it from the outside, you can walk around it and look at it. And then you can catalogue what you can know in language about it. You can catalogue how long it is, in terms of how many lines; how many stanzas it has, and how many lines are there in each stanza, and you can consider whether you think these things are relevant or not to whether it's terrific. And some of them will be and some of them won't. You can observe what the poet does at the end of the line, how he gets from the end of one line to the beginning of the next line. At the end of lines it's possible to speed up and go fast, to go quickly around the corner, or to slow down quite excessively, and come in very stately at the next turn. Something will happen at the end of lines, though, even if poems are almost in prose; unless they are in prose—if they are in verse there is a break at the end of the line. Now whether you read it or not, it's there. And it has some meaning. How much the poet is doing with what you can do at the end of lines is always very interesting. Those are some things you can look at when you're looking at poems. My favorite kinds of poems very often have been those that I hadn't much idea what they were saying at all. They were very mysterious. I just simply didn't understand. But there was some feeling, some intensity in them that spoke out directly to me, that made me suddenly feel like my light had been turned on in some way. And that I wanted to get to know the poem better. Or I wanted to get to know myself better by way of that poem. Or I wanted to get to know the world, the flesh, the devil better. I wanted to know something about something. And the best of those kind of poems for me are those poems that have stayed that way, those poems that I got to know many millions of things about and yet, when I go back to them, they're still there, like a tree, or like a bus—and it's very baffling. Again to refer you to John Ashbery, he has a poem which begins, and I'm speaking now of first lines. One of the ways that you can be interested in the writing of poetry is to be interested—and in writing terrific poems—is to be interested in how you begin. A good way to begin is in some really terrific way. There are—I like the word terrific because it has so many possible meanings, and I'm not going to pin down any of those. John Ashbery's poem *The Ecclesiast* begins, " 'Worse than the sunflower' she had said." That's the whole first line . . . and "Worse than the sunflower" is in quotes. And the poem goes on, and it's a very fine poem. I don't think I ever really understand what relationship the first line has to the rest of the poem, except it got me into it. On the other hand, to take another example a different kind of experience with a poem, there is a poem of John Ashbery's called *The Grapevine,* in his book *Some Trees,* which is one of my favorite poems of all time, and with it, I am actually at a place now, I think, where I know exactly what is being said. Word by word, the first hundred times I read it, I couldn't really understand. And so I did walk around it, and I looked at all the things that it was, how it looked, and how its shoulders were, and how its legs were and tried to see what kind of animal this was, and eventually I feel I did understand it, its meaning, the how of its meaning. It begins, this poem called *The Grapevine,* it's written on the blackboard here. This is the opening of the poem: "Of who we and all they are you all now know." I think that's about the first line and a half of the poem. And it goes very fast. And so when you first come across the poem, in the beginning, and you read it, you don't even know how to talk from about three words on. You can't pronounce anything. It says, "Of who we and all they are you all now know." And you feel like saying to that poem, now wait just a minute. I not only of who we and all they are do all not now know, but I don't even know what in the hell is going on. You know, but obviously the person speaking doesn't have time to wait. He has to get this said fairly quickly, or maybe lose it. But one thing I discovered while walking around that poem is that all those words had only one syllable in them. And so I developed a secret idea in my own head that whenever you could use a lot of words in a row with just one syllable in them, you were being terrific. And that rule has generally *held up* pretty well. In poems by adults, Frank O'Hara has a poem called *A Terrestrial Cuckoo* that begins, "What a hot day it is for Jane and me." Now those are all words with one syllable, not only that, but they have unbelievable rhyme progressing going in there, like "what, hot, for; and day," "Jane," and. And Frank's poem is a fairly stupid poem too, but it's very, it's stupid in the right way; it's *very* terrific. This next first line, also written on that blackboard, is by a poet named Jim Brodey. It's from a poem in this anthology of New York Poets. An anthology by Ron Padgett & David Shapiro. And what it says is, "Back at San Francisco Greyhound, leaning." Now what I like about that line is that the last word in it, "leaning," is what the first word, "back," is doing. Although when you read the line the first time, the word back means the other kind of back, it means I'm back here again. But when you get to the word leaning, the entire line is buzzed for a second, you understand his back is leaning against the wall, and that's possibly even what made him be able to write the poem. I've written 2900 variations on that line, none of which were ever as good as that. You could find lots of good, even terrific, lines in lots of poems that are not so good, and you could find lots of good, and even terrific poems with lots of lines in them that are not so good. That happens. That doesn't really matter so much as the fact that it is important to have *your* poems be terrific. I suppose I would qualify that, or break it down, since your poems are involved always, whether you like it or not, with who is speaking, in the poem, there are the various ways that human beings can speak, & you want to know something about yourself, if you're a person who writes down what you say. You want to know something about what you say. How do you say things in general, what would you say in any situation, how do you sound when you tell stories? You want to know that, so you can put it in your poems, . . . so that you can know all the ways that you don't sound, all your ways of sounding that you're not using in your poems; because the more aware you are of all the ways you talk, of your own sound, the more you will use them, use them naturally with ease in your poems. Then, further, you might want to write an elevated, grand-exalted poem, and you may not ever talk that way. But you can write it anyway. Because you're available, your head box contains those ways to talk, all ways to talk, even though you may never use them. You can use them when you write, because you can find the places to get that grand language. It exists in the world, you've heard it, you can stretch it.

Here is a poem by James Schuyler, a poet ten or eleven years older than I am, which would put him just into his fifties. The poem is called *Fabergé*. Fabergé was a man who made jewelry, silver & gold pieces with rubies and diamonds, opals, ivory or jade or emeralds on them, and he is a very famous maker of exotic jewelry. The poem is not about Fabergé, rather it's like a piece by Fabergé, it has lots of precious stones in it, and it has a lot of strange other things that you could put in a setting, or make a setting with. Think of a poem as a place in which you can put a lot of strange beautiful things, in strange beautiful settings. *Fabergé*. This poem is in prose, more or less. By that I mean it looks like it to me, like it's in prose, but I never think of it as being in prose. All the sentences have quotation marks around them, so that they're all statements by somebody, presumably all by the same person: there could be more than one person. That doesn't really matter yet the important thing in this is just talking and you are getting to hear. You're not being addressed so much as you're getting to hear.

FABERGÉ

I keep my diamond necklace in a pond of sparkling water for invisibility.

My rubies in Algae Pond are like an alligator's adenoids.

> My opals the evening cloud slipped in my pocket and I felt it and vice versa.
>
> Out of all the cabs I didn't take (a bit of a saver) I paved a street with gold. It was quite a short street, sort of a doll house cul-de-sac.
>
> And there are a lot of other pretties I could tell about ivory horses carved inside bone dice; coral monkeys too tiny to touch; a piece of jade so big you might mistake it for the tundra and a length of chalcedony as long as the Alcan Highway which is the Alcan Highway. It is solidified liquid chalcedony.
>
> Here, just for you, is a rose made out of a real rose and the dew drop nestled in a rosy petal that has the delicate five o'clock shadow fuzz-blue-is not a tear. I have nothing to cry about now I have you.

I'll talk about that poem a little bit. I've always liked that poem very much because I've thought of it as a poem in which the poet ever so delicately lifts the lid a little bit on the pot of boiling human and more than human living forms inside a human being's skull. It lets you see inside a head and there are many beautiful and rare stones there encased in wonderful and beautiful designs, all of which are familiar but strange. And there is danger in a delicate balance. It is so beautiful, but the terror is so naked. There is remarkable courage. I don't think that was an easy poem to write. I think it was easy to write it if you *could* write it. That is, I think he probably wrote it in about ten minutes. But I don't think that very many people could write it, or anything like it. I've always felt about poetry that you should write every poem that is given to you to write, if you can. Because if you don't write it, perhaps no one will, and those poems will be lost which none of us can afford. Life for the living of it desperately needs for every poem to exist. So what that means is that you should have a big chest of drawers in the room that you work in, in which you can leave a lot of poems which may seem to you not all that important, but it's very important that you wrote them. Because you do have a responsibility to the world, in which poems exist, if you can see poems there that could be written. You have a responsibility to write them. And if they don't turn out so well, or if they don't turn out to be so striking, if you weren't up to them at the time, that's all right, too. Yes.

Q: Are you a saver of old poems or do you keep everything you write and then sometimes you go, well, I can't think of anything to write off-hand, and then you go back and rewrite something you wrote before, and you go, well, I got this off, and then the next step is something else, you know, it might make good stew or something. Or do you think you should, like you talked about that big chest of drawers in your room, keep all the poems that you write and throw in, they aren't one hundred per cent excellent poems, just sort of ok poems, you just leave them in there, and then when you leave the room, leave the poems behind?

T.B.: No, all the poems that I write are really terrific. [*Laugh.*] No, I'm just kidding. I'm sorry, I was just thinking while you were asking that question, what would be a terrific answer that I wish I could say. But yes, I am the kind of person who saves nearly everything I write, and I write much more than poems, I rewrite lines and fragments, and I keep all those too. I make poems as much as I write them, and when I have collected a certain amount of material then I will sit down—when I have the feeling, when the feeling arises in me that I have enough material to make three or four poems, I will sit down perhaps and make one. And I'll use that material plus what comes to me from starting to put the material in the places that it should go, in the places that it indicates it should go. And sometimes the poem will consist entirely of the material I've built up, sometimes I'll only use the tiniest piece of the material and that will trigger entirely original writing at that moment. It can go in various ways. But yes I do save just about everything. I save things in different ways, that is, I have vast collection of poems that are pretty much failed poems, in the sense that they're really not very good. But they were the best I could do at that time. And in fact for that time when I wrote them they were pretty good. And I'm interested in that person who wrote those poems. And yes I have cannibalized those poems for parts of other poems. But I still keep those poems. I just keep them around, you know. In fact if I were to die tomorrow without really being dead and my editor were to whisper to me did I want all those included in my collected works, I would say yes. Because I don't, I'm not too interested in a collected works in which every poem is a totally terrific and wonderful masterpiece, 'cause that's inhuman. I like books in which every poem is a masterpiece. It's the John Ashbery way to try and have a book in which every poem is really outstanding and terrific. It's the Allen Ginsberg way not to worry about that, but to get in everything that you have around that time that is related and is above a certain level, that is, however fragmentary, or overdone, alive! John Ashbery has a great store of poems he made which I think are really very terrific, which he hasn't ever put in any books. Some of them I think are better than some of the ones in the books. But I mean that's none of my business, really. Again, besides having a collection of failed poems, I have a collection of material that's just material. That stuff has to be pretty fresh, I mean anything that's more than a couple of months, three months old, I can't really use it. It has to be on whatever is germinating in me now. I have a little address book in which I write down things that I hear all around me. I have another, larger book that I keep by the side of my bed. I like to write poems that get finished when I write them. I don't like to do much with them afterwards. My having been nurtured, educated so to speak in the age of abstract expressionism, I'm used to the gestural process of going for it the first time. And getting it there. And yet many of my poems have been rewritten many times. When I look at them hard enough, I realize how many times I had to go at them to get it right. I do advocate saving everything, yeah. Most poets do. You can periodically have a great housecleaning and throw out everything. About two months ago I threw out all the letters I received in about the last ten years. Because the alternative was either to sell them to some library, to keep them around, or put them in storage, which I couldn't afford. Oh, I suppose I could have given them back to the people, many of the people actually wept bitter tears and complained that I didn't give them back to them. Fuck them, I mean they wrote those letters to me, they should have made copies. It gave me exquisite delight to throw those letters away, actually. Because I still have them in a certain sense. But now I don't have to look at these horrifying envelopes that I used to have filled with millions of letters. I had a thought recently that I should throw away all my poetry except my published books. And then I could really see if I wanted to write any more. But I was afraid I wouldn't want to write any more, so I didn't do that. I mean I've written a lot of poetry. You write a lot of poetry in twenty years. So it gets to be a lot. I mean I have. When I moved from Chicago to New York, I had a duffel bag that weighed about one hundred pounds, full of my writings. That's a lot of writing, that's too much writing. Too much junk. But the thing is, they were all terrific. All right? Next, I want to read to you a poem by Edwin Denby. It seems to be called *Seventeen*—No, I mean it doesn't have a title, it's from a sequence, and it's *#17*. But it's also entire in itself.

17

Thin air I breathe and birds use for flying
Over and through trees standing breathing in air
Air insects drop through in insects dying
And deer that use it to listen in, share

Thickens with mist on the lake, or rain
Cuts it with tasteless water and a grey
Day colors it and it is the thin and plain
Air in my mouth, the air for miles away.

So close it feeds me each second, everyone's friend
Hugging outside and inside, I can't get rid

Of air, I know it, til the hateful end
when with it I give up the insanely hid

The airless secret I strangle not to share
With all the others as others share the air.

Edwin Denby

Now again, that's very terrific, that's a very terrific poem. And it's an honor to be alive in the same time as a man who can write a poem like that. And it's also a clue that you can write one too. Why not, I mean it was there to write in our time. That poem has some beautiful examples of accuracy in it! "Thin air I breathe." It has that beautiful Miltonic kind of inversion which everyone says you're never supposed to do. You're supposed to say, "I breathe thin air." But that's not right, if you say that. Cause you don't breathe thin air. Maybe you do. Maybe you breathe air thinly? What is it you do, I don't really know. But that's not what he's talking about, he's talking about thin air. Actually he's talking about air, but for him it's thin air.

I don't want to go on into anything further in saying that in poems what is of interest, if you're a student, is who's speaking. What kind of person is speaking to you in this poem. That could be extended into wider levels of abstraction, but I prefer to leave it right where it is. What kind of person wrote this poem? That's really what you mean when you say who is speaking. If you come up with a poem in which the person who wrote it is not the person who is speaking, that's something else, but what kind of person is speaking, who is speaking. The second thing that is of interest is who is being spoken to? Are you the general audience and the particular person, the person being spoken to, or is the person speaking speaking to someone particular and personal to themselves, or even just themself. Themself, right. That's a useful word. If you know who is speaking in any sense, you'll at least be aware that someone else is speaking. If you know what you're being spoken to, then the voice is coming at you direct. You are being spoken to, so the line is like this. Straight at you. Me to you. If the person is speaking from there, and speaking to someone else over there, and where you are is here, then you are watching it happen. And that's of some interest, where you are in relationship to who is being spoken to, and who is speaking.

And thirdly of all this, what is being said. And it's very difficult, almost impossible to know what is being said, until you have some sense of what the person speaking is like, and to whom the person is speaking. So I'm saying that content is not there to provide form. That is, form is not an extension of content. I deny that. I don't believe that it is in any way true. Form is not an extension of anything. Form and content are the same thing. Inseparable and interwoven. And you absolutely cannot say that form is an extension of content.

Bob Creeley didn't say it, in case anybody's interested. I've had long talks with him about this. He said something, and Charles Olson said, You mean that form is an extension of content? And Bob said (grunt) and Charles said, great, and then he wrote 700 essays and said, as Robert Creeley says, form is an extension of content. Form is not an extension of content.

OK, let me tack on a P.S. When Allen, since this is Allen's class, I'll say this as a loving thank you note to Allen for letting me speak in his class, when Allen was detailing the reason for, the whys and wherefores of how you put the poem on the page, in talking about the open-field poem, and how you put one part here, and one part over there, and one part down here, etc., one thing he forgot to mention was that one valid reason for putting a part of a poem anywhere on the page is because it looks beautiful and terrific there. So if you start a poem and you put some of it here, and you want to put the next part of it there, because you have a third part which you're going to put over here, because when you do it'll look beautiful and be gorgeous, and it will also be right, that's as good enough a reason as one can ever come up with. There's nothing wrong with beauty: altho it isn't necessarily better than ugliness. As William Saroyan says, "It's no help, but it's a good thing." Thank you.

Sources

ALLEN, DONALD, *The New American Poetry, 1945-60* (New York: Grove Press, 1960).

ASHBERY, JOHN, "The Ecclesiast," *Rivers and Mountains: Poems* (New York: Holt, Rinehart & Winston, 1966).

______, "The Grapevine," *Some Trees* (New Haven: Yale University Press, Corinth Books, 1970).

BRODEY, JIM, ______, *An Anthology of New York Poets,* eds. Ron Padgett and David Shapiro (New York: Random House, 1970), p. 9.

DENBY, EDWIN, "17," from *The Collected Poems of Edwin Denby,* p. 34. Used by permission of Full Court Press, New York. Copyright © 1975 by Edwin Denby.

GINSBERG, ALLEN, "Some Considerations of Mindful Arrangements of Open Verse Forms on the Page" (San Francisco: City Lights Books, 1978).

O'HARA, FRANK, "Ode to Michael Goldberg ('s Birth and Other Births)," *The Collected Poems of Frank O'Hara,* ed. Don Allen (New York: Alfred A. Knopf, Inc., 1971), pp. 297-298. Reprinted by permission of the publisher.

______, "A Terrestrial Cuckoo," op. cit., p. 24.

______, "Why I Am Not a Painter," op. cit., p. 261-262.

______, "Poem" (At Night Chinamen Jump), *Meditations in an Emergency.* Reprinted by permission of Grove Press, Inc. Copyright © 1957 by Frank O'Hara.

SCHUYLER, JAMES, "Fabergé," copyright © 1964 by Societe Anonyme d'Editions Literature et Artistiques, from *Freely Espousing* by James Schuyler. Reprinted by permission of Doubleday & Company, Inc.

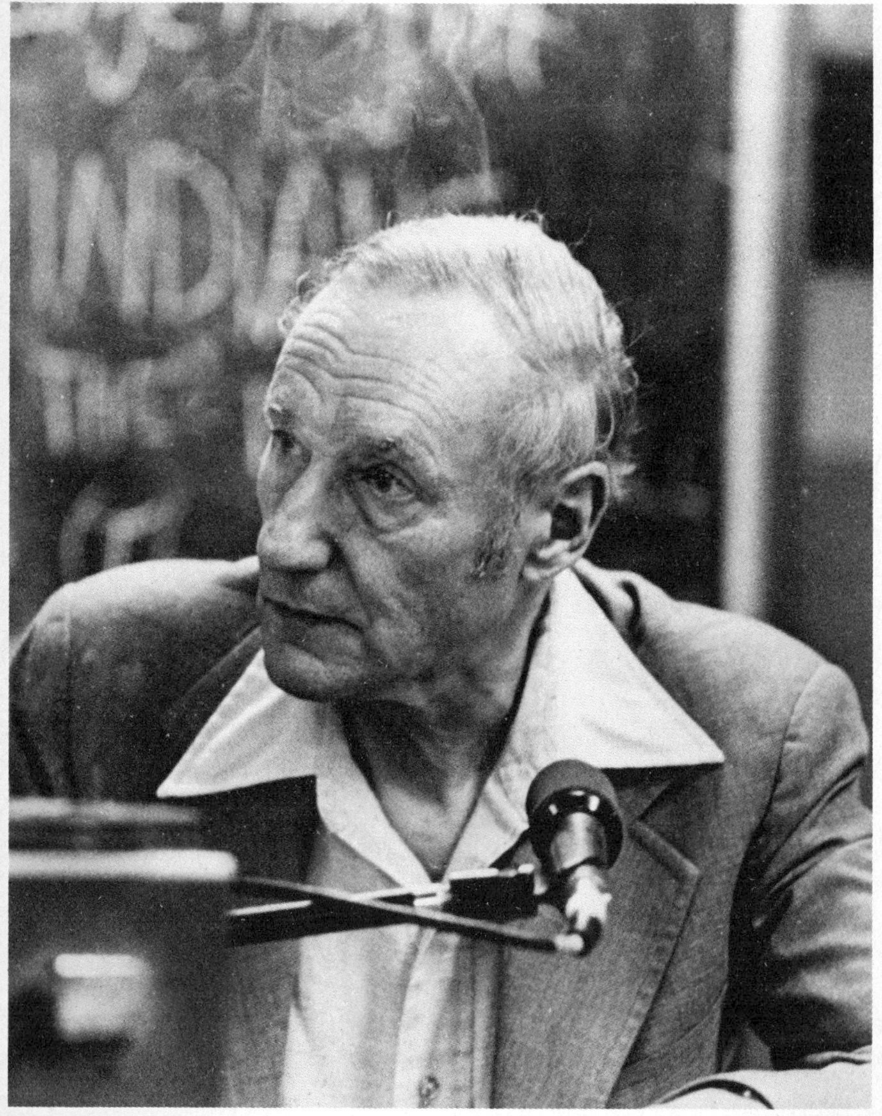

Photo by Andrea Craig

William S. Burroughs

IT BELONGS TO THE CUCUMBERS: ON THE SUBJECT OF RAUDIVE'S TAPE VOICES

JULY 27, 1976

IT SEEMS THAT tape recordings made with no apparent input have turned up unexplained voices on the tape. "Voice phenomena are done with a tape recorder and microphones set up in the usual way and using factory-fresh tape. No sounds are heard or emitted during the recording, but on replay faint voices of unknown origin appear to have been recorded" [*reads* The Handbook of Psychic Discoveries]. Visible speech diagrams and voiceprints have confirmed that these actually are recorded voices. The most complete source book on this is *Breakthrough,* by Konstantin Raudive.

These voices seem an appropriate topic to take up at the Kerouac School of Disembodied Poetics. Before discussing the experiments carried out by Raudive, I will describe experiments I performed with Brion Gysin and Ian Sommerville twelve years before *Breakthrough* was published and, in fact, before it was written. These experiments started not on tape recorders but on paper. In 1959 Brion Gysin said, "Writing is fifty years behind painting," and applied the montage technique to words on a page. These cut-up experiments appeared in *Minutes to Go,* in 1959.

Subsequently, we cut up the Bible, Shakespeare, Rimbaud, our own writing, anything in sight. We made thousands of cut-ups. When you cut and rearrange words on a page, new words emerge. And words change meaning. The word "drafted," as into the Army, moved into a context of blueprints or contracts gives an altered meaning. New words and altered meanings are implicit in the process of cutting up, and could have been anticipated. Other results were not expected. When you experiment with cut-ups over a period of time, some of the cut and rearranged texts seem to refer to future events. I cut up an article written by John Paul Getty and got: "It is a bad thing to sue your own father." And a year later one of his sons did sue him. In 1964 I made a cut-up and got what seemed at the time a totally inexplicable phrase: "And there is a horrid air conditioner." In 1974 I moved into a loft with a broken air conditioner, which was removed to put in a new unit. And there were three hundred pounds of broken air conditioner on my floor—a horrid disposal problem, heavy and solid, emerged from a cut-up ten years ago.

The next step was cut-ups on the tape recorder. Brion was the first to take this obvious step. A step becomes obvious when someone takes it. Like five hundred years of cannonballs before someone got the idea of a cannonball that explodes on contact—American Civil War. From that point a series of steps led to long-range artillery and intercontinental missiles. Why does it take so long for such obvious developments? Perhaps because the way is blocked by preconceptions. The first tape recorder cut-ups were a simple extension of cut-ups on paper. You record, say, ten minutes on the recorder. Then you spin the reel backwards or forwards without recording. Stop at random and cut in a phrase. How random is random? We know so much that we don't consciously know we know, that perhaps the cut-in was not random. The operator on some level knew just where he was cutting in, just as you know on some level exactly where you were and what you were doing ten years ago at this precise moment. Cut-ups put you in touch with what you know and do not know that you know. Of course this procedure on the tape recorder produces new words by altered juxtaposition just as new words are produced by cut-ups on paper.

We went on to exploit the potentials of the tape recorder: cut up, slow down, speed up, run backwards, inch the tape, play several tracks at once, cut back and forth between two recorders. As soon as you start experimenting with slowdowns, speedups, overlays, etc., you will get new words that were not on the original recordings. There are then many ways of producing words and voices on tape that did not get there by the usual recording procedure, words and voices that are quite definitely and clearly recognizable by a consensus of listeners.

I have gotten words and voices from barking dogs. No doubt one could do much better with dolphins (which does not mean that the dolphins have mastered the English language). And words will emerge from recordings of dripping faucets. In fact, almost any sound that is not too uniform may produce words. Every little breeze seems to whisper Louise. The very tree branches brushing against her window seemed to mutter murder murder murder. Well, the branches may have muttered just that, and you could hear it back with a recorder. Everything you hear and see is there for you to hear and see it. So that people may think they are losing their minds when they find that what they see and hear in the street has a personal meaning for them. Some time ago a young man came to see me and said he was going mad. Street signs, overheard conversations, radio broadcasts seemed to refer to him in some way. I told him, "Of course they refer to you. *You* see and hear them."

You can scan a word out of a foreign language of which you don't know a word, and let me confess that I do not know a word of Arabic, taking refuge for my failings as a linguist in George Bernard Shaw, who said that he who is at home in his own language will not be at home in any other. Years ago, Ian Sommerville, Stewart Gordon, and your reporter had turned into the Rue des Vignes, just off the Place de France, in Tangier. Walking ahead of us was a middle-aged Arab couple, obviously poor country people down from the mountains. And one turned to the other and said: "WHAT ARE YOU GOING TO DO?"

We all heard it. Perhaps the Arab words just happened to sound like that. Perhaps it was a case of consensual scanning. I had a friend who went "mad" in Tangier. He was scanning out personal messages from Arab broadcasts. This is the more subjective phenomenon of personal scanning patterns. I say "more" rather than pose the either/or, subjective/objective alternative, since all phenomena are both subjective *and* objective. He was, after all, listening to radio broadcasts.

Now to consider Raudive's experimental procedure. The experiments were carried out in a soundproof studio. A new blank tape was turned on and allowed to record. Then the tape was played back, the experimenter listening through headphones, and quite recognizable voices and words were found to be recorded on the tape.

Raudive has recorded 100,000 phrases of these voices. The speech is almost double the usual speed, and the sound is pulsed in rhythms like poetry or chanting. These voices are in a number of accents and languages, often quite ungrammatical . . . "You I friends. Where stay?" Sounds like a Tangier hustler. Reading through the sample voices in *Breakthrough,* I was struck by many instances of a distinctive style reminiscent of schizophrenic speech, certain dream utterances, some of the cut-ups and delirium voices like the last words of Dutch Schultz. Many of the voices allegedly come from the dead. Hitler, Nietzsche, Goethe, Jesus Christ, anybody who is anybody is there, many of them having undergone a marked deterioration of their mental and artistic faculties. Goethe isn't what he used to be. Hitler had a bigger and better mouth when he was alive. On one level the recorded voices' procedure is a form of sophisticated electronic table-tapping, and table-tapping is one aspect of the cut-up experiments I have described. What better way to contact someone than to cut and rearrange his actual words? Certainly an improvement on the usual scene where Shakespeare is announced to be followed by some excruciatingly bad poetry. Whether there is actual contact with the dead is an academic question so long as there is no way to prove or disprove it.

Messages from the dead or not, the voices frequently refer to the thoughts and preoccupations of those present at the session or to people connected with those present. Here is an example from *The Handbook of Psychic Discoveries* (p. 226) :

> New experiments began with a surprise. The German team lost their way. At the same time one of the group was stricken with a very severe toothache. Meanwhile, Jurgenson decided to try a recording session on his own. Replaying the tape he heard the German words, "Sie kommen bald. Zahnartz. Zahnartz"; They will arrive soon. Dentist. Dentist.

I have pointed out a stylistic similarity between the voices recorded by Raudive, dream speech, schizophrenic speech, words spoken in delirium, and cut-ups. This does not apply to all the material in these categories, much of which may be quite banal and undistinguished. For example, a frequently recurring phrase in Raudive's book is "Heat the bathroom, company is coming (p. 139) ." This is no esoteric code, but simply refers to a Latvian custom. When they are expecting guests, someone goes into the bathroom and lights the stove. It is a question of selecting material which is stylistically interesting, or which may contain references of personal or prophetic significance. I have already given some examples of cut-ups. Here are some examples of dream speech: "We can come out when shadows cover the cracks." This is from one of my students at City College of New York, who encountered Hemingway in a dream and asked him how he could be there if he was dead. That was Hemingway's reply. And from my own dream diaries:

> You need black money here. We still don't have the nouns. Do you like to get lost or patrol cars? The symbol of the skull and the symbol of soap turn on the same axis. Can't you keep any ice? The Inspectorate of Canada is banging on the door. I suppose you think Missouri is a lump. You have an airforce appetite. The lair of the bear is in Chicago. The unconscious imitated by cheesecake. A tin of tomato soup in Arizona. Where naked troubadours shoot snotty baboons. Green is a man to fill is a boy. I can take the hut set anywhere. A book called *Advanced Outrage.* An astronaut named Platt. First American shot on Mars. Life is a flickering shadow with violence before and after it. A good loser always gives up control for what the situation would be if control wasn't there to look around in it.

And here are two examples of dream slang: an ounce of heroin is a "beach." "To camel" is dream slang for "fuck." Unfortunately I do not have examples of schizophrenic speech (and collecting this material would be a very useful project). I remember only two: "Doctorhood is being made with me." Stylistically similar to the Inspectorate of Canada. And: "Radius radius . . . it is enough."

A few quotes from the last words of Dutch Schultz:

> The glove will fit what I say. I wanted to break the ring, I get a month. He was a cowboy in one of the seven days a week fight. In the olden days they waited and they waited. Let me in the district. Please let me get in and eat. That is something that should not be spoken about. Be instrumental in letting us know. No. It is confused and it says no. A boy has never wept nor dashed a thousand kim. Please crack down on the Chinaman's friends and Hitler's commander. Mother is the best bet and don't let Satan draw you too fast. They are French people. It was desperate. I am wobbly. I don't want harmony/I want harmony. Open this up and

break it so I can touch you. The baron says these things. Come on open the soap duckets. The chimney-sweeps take to the sword. French Canadian bean soup. I want to pay. Let them leave me alone.

Here are some phrases from Raudive's book. I have taken these phrases out of what might be called minimal context for purposes of illustration:

> Cheers here are the nondead. Here are the cunning ones. We are here because of you. We are all longing to go home. Politics, here is death. Take the grave with you. It snows horribly. We see Tibet with the binoculars of the people. Give reinforcement. Diminish the stopper. Sometimes only the native country loves. I am expensive. We are coordinated, the guard is manifold. You belong probably to the cucumbers. Telephone with restraint comrade. It is difficult in Train A. Covering fire. Send orders. Are you without jewelry? A lecture is taking place here. We have become accustomed to our sick ones. Get out of the defensive position. Speed is required. Leave it in full gear. Have done with the seemingly apparent. Please to use studio postulated to you. Faustus, good morning. I demand our authorities. This is the aunt's language. Identity card. Passport. Bind death, obey death. Bring a halibut. You can refuse. It is permitted. A pistol is our man. This is operational. Even the wolves do not stay here. Into battle. The long life flees. We ignite. It is bad here. Here the birds burn. It smells of the operational death. Knowledgeable Goth, the deed of the future. Believe. Separated. Here is eternity. The far away exists. You are the contract. Are you in salt? We have been looking all over the place for human beings. Ah good the sea. Professor of non-existence, the body is evidence of the spirit. The natural key. We are the language here. The doctor is on the market. Good evening our chap, are you making mummies to standard? It is

> enough. Reason submitted. Called at a bad time. This is operational even in the middle. With binoculars at the border, you have nevertheless to fetch our clothes. Prepare trousers in the bathroom. Why are you a German? Clean out the earth. The new Germany. Hitler is a good animal-infesting louse. Have you stolen horse with him? *Yo siento.* Man pricks. *Buena cosa* man. Draw the spirit to the *plata.* Hurry to make the flutes. Facts see us. I am practically here. A good crossing. The earth disintegrated.

Commentary: "We see Tibet with the binoculars of the people." In 1970, about the time that these recordings were made, I wrote a story about a Chinese patrol who finds a Tibetan monastery taken over by the CIA to test a radioactive virus. The first lines are:

> The scouting party stopped a few hundred yards from the village on the bank of a stream. Yen Lee studied the village through his field glasses while his men sat down and lit cigarettes.

"You belong probably to the cucumbers." I don't know how many of you are familiar with a term used to designate the CIA: "the pickle factory." "He works for the pickle factory" means he is a CIA man. I think this designation was mentioned in *Time* or *Newsweek.* I had already heard it from CIA acquaintances. Well, pickles are made from cucumbers, so it doesn't seem too far-fetched to postulate that "cucumbers" refers to the CIA.

"Telephone with restraint comrade." Watch what you say over the phone—the cucumbers are listening in.

"Bind death. Obey death." Compare to Dutch Schultz's last words, "I don't want harmony. I want harmony."

"Are you in salt? We have been looking all over the place for human beings." Salt could refer to any basic commodity. In this case, since the voices are discarnate, the reference is probably to human bodies. Your blood as you know has the saline content of sea water —"Ah good the sea." Now, to say "Are you in blood?" would blow the vampiric cover.

"Have you stolen horse with him?" is a German proverb meaning "can you trust him?"

"Draw the spirit to the *plata*." Raudive considers this utterance inexplicable. Apparently he did not know that *plata* is a general Spanish slang term for money.

"A good crossing. The earth disintegrated." Some years ago scientists drew up a plan for a space ship to be propelled by atomic blasts behind it. Well, that would be a motive for blowing up the earth: propulsion to healthier areas.

The publication of *Breakthrough* in England caused quite a stir. One of the editors, Peter Bander, later published a book entitled *Voices From the Tapes,* describing the reactions in England. There were articles in the press, radio and television programs, much discussion pro and con. Some people protested that if these are voices from the dead, they seem to be living not in celestial realms but in a cosmic hell. In consequence the voices may be misleading, interested, even downright ill-intentioned. Well, what did they expect? A chorus of angels with tips on the stock market? Others protested that contact with these voices is dangerous, citing the use of black magic and the invocation of lower astral entities by Nazi leaders. An article written by a psychic researcher, Gordon Turner, typifies the "dangerous for the uninitiated" line. Turner's article was written in answer to an article by someone named Cass, in which Cass says: "If a door has been opened between this world and the next, then the masses, armed with their cheap transister sets and five-pound Hong Kong recorders, will participate despite Gordon Turner, the Pope, and the Government."

Here is Turner: "I believe *Breakthrough* should not have been published. Does [*Cass*] think it is safe for anyone and everyone to open themselves to this kind of influence? Has he the slightest conception of how dangerous this might be?" Dangerous to whom exactly? When people start talking about the danger posed by making psychic knowledge available to the masses, they are generally trying to monopolize this knowledge for themselves. In my opinion, the best safeguard against the abuse of such knowledge is wide dissemination. The more people that know about it, the better. The time has come to dump all these secrets on the table. Secret weapons, secret doctrines, the lot. They are less dangerous in the hands of the general public than in the hands of intelligence agencies and the military. Knowledge belongs to anyone who can use it.

Now to combine the tape recorder experiments already described with Raudive's procedure. Raudive's recordings were made in a soundproof studio. He was concerned with demonstrating that the voices were recorded under controlled conditions and could not be attributed to accidental background sounds or voices, people talking in the street, a radio broadcast next door, or people talking in the studio. And I think that anyone who examines the evidence will agree that he has proved his case.

So I am not interested simply in collecting additional proof, but in the actual phenomenon on tape, whatever its source. A soundproof studio is not essential. In fact, the first to pick up on the voices in 1959 was a Swedish painter, Friedrich Jurgenson, who was recording bird songs. On playing back his recordings of bird songs, he heard a quiet male voice discussing nocturnal bird songs in Norwegian. And Jurgenson was the one who turned Raudive on to the voices.

The first step would be to take Raudive's recordings and process them—speed up, slow down, cut up, scramble—and see what new words and voices emerge. I will perform these experiments as soon as I can get the record he has put out, a record of the actual recordings. Meanwhile, I have done some simple cut-ups on paper and on the recorder, using my own voice reading his recorded phrases. This is only a beginning. Now let us say that you are invoking Rimbaud. Instead of working with the whole tape blank, you prerecord on another recorder a few phrases of Rimbaud's poems and cut them in during the recording, at random. On playback pay particular attention to the fraction of a second before and after the prerecording cuts in. You can use the same procedure with any writer living or dead. In the case of musicians or singers, music or singing can be cut in in this way. Or in cases where recordings of someone's voice exist, these could be used.

There are many variations. During the recording, project a film without the sound track and see if any of the sound track finds its way onto the tape. You could read silently Shakespeare, Rimbaud, the Bible, *Newsweek,* and see if there is any correlation between this reading and the tape. You all know how a tune can stick in your head and play over and over—would such compulsive subvocal playback be picked up on tape? Hearing voices is a diagnostic indication of schizophrenia; could these voices be picked up on tape in the vicinity of psychotic patients?

Raudive considers three theories to account for the voices: 1) They are somehow imprinted on the tape by electromagnetic energy generated by the unconscious minds of the researchers or people connected with them. 2) The voices are of extraterrestrial origin. 3) The voices come from the dead. He then crosses out number one, the imprint theory, because it is "technically impossible." It seems to me that we are operating in an area where technical impossibilities, in terms of what we know about magnetic tape and the way in which sounds and voices are imprinted by the usual means, no longer apply. We could make tapes where the participants concentrate on imprinting certain voices. Suppose we take twenty Kerouac students who have read his novels, heard his voice on tape, seen photos of him at various ages. They all gather in the studio silently, concentrating on Kerouac. Would this have any effect on the content of the tape? Even a high correlation, the recording for example of voices purporting to come from Kerouac, would not prove that the voices are imprinted by concentration, conscious or unconscious, or those present; but it would suggest that the voices might be *influenced* in this way. Remember that your memory bank contains tapes of everything you have ever heard, including of course your own words. Press a certain button, and a news broadcast you heard ten years ago plays back. There is ample proof of this vertiginous warehouse of data stored in the human nervous system, and no method of passing it along for disposal has so far been devised. Under hypnosis, people have remembered in detail conversations and events that took place many years ago, and this has been confirmed by witnesses.

Hypnotic subjects have been able to recall exactly what doctors and nurses said during an operation, and such recall, particularly if it has a menacing or derogatory content, can be extremely disturbing . . .

"One thing is sure—he don't look good."

"A filthy mess . . ."

"Sew her up, it's inoperable."

"Clamps, nurse, he's bleeding like a pig."

"Prepare the patient for a heart shot."

"A round of drinks he dies on the table."

These irresponsible observations are recorded and stored in the patient's memory bank, enough to convey a permanent patient status. In Esquire's 1971 Christmas issue, there is an article called "Future Shock"; Doctor Cheek, who carried out hypnotic experiments on post-operative subjects and found they were recording every word and sound in the operating room, recommended that silence be observed during an operation. Because what the patient hears during an operation is filed with all his tapes of pain, fear, helplessness and hostility—all the horrible, frightening, disgusting things he has ever known awake or asleep, conscious or unconscious, from his conception.

You know the old joke about the couple who adopted a French baby, taking French lessons so they would understand him when he started to talk. Like many jokes, it's not a joke. Doctor Truby has found that children adopted at birth by parents speaking a different language may be retarded in consequence, since they have heard and stored the mother's language in the womb. Years of tapes recorded day and night are stored in your memory bank, and films to go with them in most cases. Talkies, Feelies, Smellies, Tasties, and any of these tapes can be activated by touching an associational switch. You are walking down the street and something you see, hear, smell, turns on an old tape you haven't heard in twenty years—"Now why did I think of that?" Everyone you have ever known, however briefly, is there on film and tape. Take a look at these talking films and you will begin to notice that certain words and characters tend to recur. The rude clerk in Hong Kong bore a strong resemblance to the rude clerk in New York, and both used the same words to indicate they did not have what you asked for: "I never heard of it."

The more you look at it, the more it looks like a tired old film, nice voices, nasty voices, good guys and bad guys, the old game of war from the Stone Age to eternity . . .

"Are we men or toothless crones? How long will we allow the filthy Zambesi to plunder our fishing territories?"

"As free men we cannot stand idly by"; time to get yourself hid good and the deeper the better. "And I say to Russia, beware the fury of a patient man." A good crossing. The earth disintegrated. Old war tapes. We all have millions of hours of it, even if we never fired a gun. War tapes, hate tapes, fear tapes, pain tapes, happy tapes, sad tapes, funny tapes, all stirring around in a cement mixer of voices.

Raudive dismisses the second alternative explanation for the origin of the voices—that they are extraterrestrial—because they are too banal. No reason to think we have a monopoly on banality.

His reason exemplifies the error of either/or thinking. Having categorically crossed out 1) and 2), he is stuck with Number 3: the voices come from the dead. I could suggest other possible explanations: The voices are a playback of recordings stored in the memory banks of the experimenters. Or why not all three, and the others he hasn't thought of, in various combinations?

Now the psychiatrists tell us with little more evidence than their words—"informed medical opinion" they call it—that any voices anyone hears in their head originate there, and that they do not and cannot have an extraneous origin. The whole psychiatric dogma that voices are the imaginings of a sick mind, has been called into question by voices which are of extraneous origin and are objectively and demonstrably there on tape. So the psychotic patients may be tuning in to a global and intergalactic network of voices, some using sophisticated electronic equipment. It belongs probably to the cucumbers. Fifteen years ago in Norway, experiments indicated that voices could be projected directly into the brain of the subject by an electromagnetic field around the head. The experiments were in a formative stage at that time. So maybe we are all walking around under a magnetic dome of prerecorded word and image, and Raudive and the other experimenters simply plugging into the prerecording.

The theory of a prerecorded universe is venerable, and many people have believed in it; especially those on the way up believe in their "destiny" as they call it. The Arab conception of fate: *Mektoub,* it is written. It goes back to the Mayan control calendar; it is written. And what is it written on? No doubt some material similar to magnetic tape, but infinitely more sophisticated. This attempt to predict by controlling and to control by predicting is very old. It can now be computerized. Such modern controllers as Hearst and Luce set out to be the prerecorded universe or as much of it as they could prerecord. Wittgenstein says no system may include itself as data; the only thing not prerecorded in a prerecorded universe is the prerecordings themselves. Or to put it another way: The only thing not predetermined in a predetermined universe is the Predeterminer. So of course we are listening to prerecordings of prerecordings to infinity. However, by listening to and processing a prerecording, you nullify its impact as a control instrument. What might have shocked your grandmother into a cataleptic state is dismissed with a weary shrug by teenagers. Think of my WASP grandmother, the wife of a circuit-riding Georgia minister, W.C.T.U., Colonial Dame, forced to witness a pornographic film.

Well, don't blame Grandma. In actuality, the change didn't happen all at once, but by a series of gradient steps. In time, as any data is widely disseminated by the media, it loses its shock impact. So then the machine has to feed you the prerecording above that—and on back, on an infinite tapeworm to the final prerecordings or prerecorders which must exist somewhere in some form. "Prerecordings to the people!" If the recordings so far received are in any way derivative from the original prerecordings—and they must be, come to think about it—then the experiment is worth your time. Peter Bander considers the voices as important a discovery as nuclear physics.

Could you, by cutting up, overlaying, scrambling, cut and nullify the prerecordings of your own future? Could the whole prerecorded future of the human race be nullified or altered? I don't know . . . let's see. And don't let any smooth old voices ease you out of it . . . "There are certain things my son that human beings are not permitted to know—" *Like what we are doing*—"Son you'd fall dead from one whiff of the pickle factory and other similar factories in other countries." Scramble him like an egg before he hatches. What is this? His hand is one of the unbearable mysteries and the other players can't see his cards, as he rakes in the chips and then says the chips are his cards, a billion on the board.

Someone asked at the last session what the tape voices have to do with poetics. Answer: Everything. Writers work with words and voices just as painters work with colors. An important point here is the misconception that a writer creates in a vacuum using only his very own words. Was he blind deaf and illiterate from birth? A writer does not own words any more than a painter owns colors. So let's dispense with this "originality" fetish. Is a painter committing plagiarism if he paints a mountain that other painters have painted? Even if he paints a mountain from another painter's painting of a mountain?

Writers work with words and voices and where do these words and voices come from? From many sources:

Conversations heard and overheard, movies and radio broadcasts, newspapers, magazines, yes, and *other writers;* a phrase comes into his mind from an old western story in a pulp magazine he read years ago, can't remember where or when: "He looked at her trying to read her mind. But her eyes were old, unbluffed, unreadable." There's one that I lifted. All writers are plagiarists. Steal anything in sight. Or a phrase comes to him and he doesn't even remember that he read it somewhere, or heard it somewhere. The County Clerk sequence in *Naked Lunch* derived from contact with the County Clerk in Cold Spring, Texas. It was in fact an elaboration of his monologue, which seemed merely boring at the time, since I didn't know yet that I was a writer. In any case, there wouldn't have been any County Clerk if I had been sitting on my ass waiting for my very own words.

You've all met the ad man who is going to get out of the rat race, shut himself up in a cabin, and write the Great American Novel. I always tell him "Don't cut your input, B.J., you might need it." So many times I have been stuck on a story line, can't see where it will go from here; then someone drops around and tells me about fruit-eating fish in Brazil. I got a chapter out of that. Or I buy a book to read on the plane, and there is the answer; and there's a nice phrase too, "sweetly inhuman voices." I had a dream about such voices before I read *The Big Jump* (Leigh Brackett) and found that phrase. In my next novel I will, as far as my memory serves, identify all the sources just to show what a patchwork of bits and pieces a novel is.

So what you pick up—and don't be ashamed to boost right and left from reading and conversations—is one source. Another source is dreams. I get about forty percent of my sets and characters from dreams. Sometimes just a phrase, a voice, a glimpse. And sometimes I will get a whole story or passage; all I have to do is sit down and transcribe the dream. An example is a story in *Exterminator!* called, "They Do Not Always Remember." And sometimes in dreams I find a book or a magazine and read a story.

Another source of material for the writer is the voices

which he is hearing all the time, whether he knows it or not. He may think he is hearing his very own words. If the tape recorder picks up the voices, so do you. A tape recorder is just a model of one function of the human nervous system. Consider the voices as a source of material for writing. Ask yourself: "Who could have said that? What does he look like? What is the context?" As the voices say, "Get out of the defensive position." Look, listen, and transcribe—and forget about being original.

I have spoken of the stylistic similarity between the voices recorded by Raudive and certain phrases we hear in dreams. The dream process goes on all the time, but is not ordinarily perceptible when you are awake, owing to sensory input and necessity of orienting yourself in an apparently objective context. The dream voices, which may well have the same sources as the voices Raudive has recorded, can be contacted at any time. It is simply necessary to put aside defensive mechanisms. The best writing is achieved in an egoless state. The writer's defensive, limited ego, his "very own words," these are his least interesting source.

The assignment for this class is to put together a page or two, or as many as you like, containing no words of your own. These can come from any source: passages of actual dialogue, books, films; anything that anybody else said. You can cut it up or rearrange it in any way you like. You can also use any dream phrases from your own or anybody else's dream, or any voices that you may have heard in your head. You can cut up material on a tape recorder and transcribe it. And I would recommend this procedure for any of you who have tape recorders available.

Here is a cut-up tape made of Raudive's voices, dream voices, cut-ups from *Minutes to Go,* Dutch Schultz's last words, all cut in with this lecture:

> Professor of non-existence, there are no pure smoked foods. Spirit is already going on your side. What you are I leave free. The connection is distance of the wolf. The native country loves. I am in sail in mother's jour-

nal. The guard is manifold. Why can refuse. It is permitted. Are cunning ones. *Yo siento.* That is our law. We miss man. Madrid I feel. We have bird's bed burn. Diminish the defensive. This is operational, even to the cucumbers. Tele reinforcements. Can you keep up with tech in train A? Covering fire. Home. Please to choose a good animal-infesting louse. Is police. We are the language. Kosti is without evening. You natural key. The doctor is midnight. A good crossing, beings. Are you in salt? Eskilis naked here. Mother at a bad time. You know, taking place here. Knowledgeable stolen horses. Seemingly fate decrees. *Var sien wend?* Body is evidence of the film. The thoughts on this side. Making the thoughts on this side. Steaming crossing point. Obey death. Bring a halibut. You are German. A pistol is our man. I am naked pricks. *Buena cosa.* The birch trees here. Accustomed to our sick stopper. You had a lack of joy position. You belong. Wolves do not stay here. Give phone with restraint comrade. Minus here in the uncertainty. Many sparks send orders. Hitler is studio postulated to you. Who are you without jewelry? It is almost on the market. All over the place for human thank you. Reason submitted. Cal is permitted. Lecture is the machine. The medicine is deed of the future.

Sources

BANDER, PETER, *Voices from the Tapes* (New York: Drake Publishers, Inc., 1973).

Ibid. Excerpt from an article by R.A. Cass from *Psychic News,* May, 1971.

Ibid. Excerpt from an article by Gordon Turner, "Raudive Voices: References to Hitler are Dangerous," op. cit.

BURROUGHS, WILLIAM, *Exterminator!* (New York: Viking Press, 1973).

———, *The Last Words of Dutch Schultz* (New York: Viking Press, 1975).

———, *Naked Lunch* (New York: Grove Press, 1959).

———, "Virus B-23 Yen Lee Story." First appeared in *Mayfair* magazine in the early 1970s.

OSTRANDER, SHEILA and SCHROEDER, LYNN, "Your Tape Recorder a Tracking Station for Paranormal Voices," *The Handbook of Psychic Discoveries* (Berkeley: Berkeley Medalion, 1975).

RAUDIVE, KONSTANTIN, *Breakthrough* (New York: Taplinger Publishing Co., 1971).

Photo by John Barkin

Edward Dorn

STRUMMING LANGUAGE

JUNE 8, 1977

I'D LIKE TO start off speaking about my sense of language, qualified by some of the things I've already heard. I don't want to bring it up again, but I do because it's interesting to me, the word *discipline,* [*as being discussed at faculty and administration gatherings*]. As it was being mulled over, I kept hearing this line from an old tune which goes,

> Reading and writing and 'rithmetic,
> all to the tune of a hickory stick.

Do you remember that? Everybody's heard it. I think actually it doesn't say so much about punishment as it does about a certain indisputable pain involved in learning certain things, and therefore has to do with drill and the relative boredom of fixed and unvarying attention, which nevertheless results in a certain kind of exactness of recall and adaptability. In the system in which I operate, reading and writing are very closely bound together metaphorically, like the spin axis of an electron-proton in atomic hydrogen.

In the light of that, I'd like to read a few short numbers from the article fifty-six from Wittgenstein, *On Uncertainty.*

> When one says perhaps this planet doesn't exist, and the light phenomenon arises in some other way, then after all one needs an example of an object which does exist. This doesn't exist, as for example does ellipsis. Or, are we to say that certainty is merely a constructed point to which some things approximate more, some less closely. No, doubt gradually loses its sense. This language game *is* like that. And everything descriptive of a language game is part of logic.

And, article fifty-eight:

> If I know (and so forth) is conceived as a grammatical proposition, of course the I cannot be important. And it properly means there is no such thing as doubt in this case. Or the expression I do not know makes no sense in this case. And, of course it follows from this that I know makes no sense either.

And article fifty-nine:

> I know is here a logical insight. Only realism can't be proved by means of it.

And article sixty-one goes:

> A meaning of a word is a kind of employment of it. For it is what we learn when the word is incorporated into our language.

When we think of English as a world language, which it is, it's used by everyone potentially, and it serves as something actually more than a grand Esperanto, simply because, not being a synthetic language it has greater possibilities of use, and relates to other living languages in a very real and direct way, and therefore, to flow in and out of it is natural. In other words, it's not a jargon to merely trade with. When one thinks of English as a world language, then its interest is precisely in its possibilities of incorporating a larger conceptualization for mankind during this era. It's a world language precisely because of its hybridization and that's an old story.

What that means for writing in our hemisphere is that Spanish has a very direct access to English, and in fact we know now that there's a very interesting body of literature growing up called "Spanglish" not practiced by that many people, but practiced increasingly well and provocatively by several people. This is to be distinguished from the kinds of margins of slang that go on between languages. It's a real incorporation. Ernesto Cardinal, for instance, is interesting in that sense and Victor Hernandez Cruz is who I'm really thinking about. He takes it most seriously. On this side, speaking of American English, it's important to think about these things, because Spanish, for instance, is the language spoken by the majority of inhabitants in this hemisphere, so that in this context English is, statistically at least, a secondary language.

There are other aspects of this condition, for instance, the imperialism of English as a language. This would be felt most sharply, I suppose, by some people like the French, who have another attitude about language. And how it's to be used. You remember, they always said that their language was diplomatic, and their paranoia is specifically that it *not* be expanded, that it not be "corrupted," that it not be diluted in that sense. But then of course the language of diplomacy is exclusive and contractual and secret. So in that way, English bears the burden of democracy more than any other instrumentation that I know of. It's important in that sense—back to the use of new terms to redefine a structure that had been motivated by other terms—to keep in mind that it's important for the language to be allowed to generate its own definitions, deliberately and spontaneously.

And it's important to avoid nominalization, that is, the creation of noun tones which don't really have any linguistic meaning in back of them, like "nowness" or the business of "isness." This is specifically a danger of people who come into an instrumentation like English and see its evident and immediate widespread uses for their own purposes, without participating in the implied democracy that English supports in the world. We say that we're the Free World, and if we don't mean that, we're crazy. The language has to mean that also. Of course that's a danger for the language. Any language takes a risk by leaving itself open to new constructions and to uncontrolled usage. Now that's by way of preamble to what I want to say about how I work.

To a certain extent my interest in the extreme heterogenous vocabularies of English is fanatical. I "think" I need a large rush of data coming in all the time. I like the media in that respect. I spend a lot of the day monitoring the flow of news and so forth, watching how the language is being used. But the way in which these contexts fold in on themselves and overlap and disappear at the margins and so forth is interesting, and since I myself don't have those classical kinds of habits of writing, which have always been said to be precise times of day and constancy, I tend to float until the pressure says I have something I want to say badly enough to stop monitoring the news. There's another kind of metaphorical way that I could also put it. It's like a buzzard; I'm the meat hanging on the bone. Or like a dog, taking the trash out of the water. It's a good service, it cleans up the landscape. And it's honorable; nobody ever bothers a buzzard or a dog. (A working dog, not a curb dog.) I think the function is aesthetically unquestionable.

Now, as an example of what I'm saying, I'm going to read from a postcard I received on the eleventh of February, 1976. It isn't addressed to me, it's just, I mean it is *addressed* to me, but I mean the salutation isn't to me. It begins,

> Law Report: Dallas City Ordinance #12991, adopted July 20, 1970 provides: It shall be unlawful for any person to loiter (include (s) the following activities: the walking about aimlessly without apparent purpose, lingering, hanging around, lagging behind, the idle spending of time, delaying, sauntering and moving slowly

> about, where such conduct is not due to physical defect or conditions. Supreme Court refused to entertain challenge because of procedural defects. Ellis and Love vs. Dyson, 95S Court 1691 1975.

I read that in relation to the Wittgenstein quotations. And one more preliminary matter, two more, three more. I just wrote this as a message to you because Allen Ginsberg bought some typewriters and was gracious enough to let me use one: I find it necessary to have a continuous stream of data pouring into my daily life and even that's not enough. For example, this morning, I opened up the case on an unfamiliar typewriter, a rather nice old Smith Corona, and was shocked to see the return lever on the left side, and muttered, "My God! This is a left-handed typewriter." It might be the altitude.

Now one of the consequences of paying attention, perhaps inordinate attention, to the ebb and flow of language is that, for me at least, the language tends to disappear, because that behavior, that attitude, that relationship to the language, tends to reduce the language. It's a refining process, it tends to make the language granular, and for me recently it's resulted in shorter and shorter pieces of expression, which I'm not interested in calling anything, and I don't mean poems, but I mean anything. And yet I'm interested in formulating what the function of them might be, so one of the masses of material I have, I'm calling *Flywheel Programs,* in that sense. And last night Gregory Corso whispered a poem to me, because apparently, I mean, I have the feeling that he is verbalizing a lot more than actually committing anything to paper now—although he didn't say that—but when I asked him if it were true, he didn't say no. This is what he said: "I can disappear before your eyes, killing you." I think that's devastating. "I can disappear before your eyes, killing you." Well, I thought that was like what I was talking about as a Flywheel Program, but at the time I thought—that's a Spansule—and I had never thought anything was a Spansule like that, before that moment, so this small mechanism prompted me to think about it in a way I'd never thought about it before, which is, I think, an extremely important function of language. And I'm increasingly thinking it might be *the* function of language.

An example of what I mean, of my own, is called *Distraction Control:* "The most ecological way to kill fleas is to kill the dog." [*Laughter.*] The point is, it's not the content so much, but where the content might lead one. I mean that in an analogical way. A flywheel is a simple mechanism whose principle is that, once it's started, once its inertia is overcome, its continuance is generated by a very low energy. That's its point, that's its mechanical efficiency. It's hard to start, easy to maintain. It's a very old, early Industrial Revolution piece of brilliant, revolutionary engineering, the flywheel. It is essentially off balance. I mean something so simple as Walt Whitman, on the one hand, and Emily Dickinson, on the other.

Ok, now I think I'll speak about how I put my notebooks together. This particular notebook I have with me today, and the one I'm going to look at and describe to you, I began in January of 1976. And the occasion was my going to La Jolla, the University of California at San Diego, which is at La Jolla. I went there to teach a quarter, from January to March, and began a book of poems, not poems, I began a book of these short expressions called "Hello La Jolla," and I got the title the first day. The text starts out with a racing ticket from Golden Gate, the third race: there's a ticket from the Paramount theater in Oakland, Bob Marley and the Whalers, a picture of Heidegger who died around that time, a little bit later, actually; a U.S. Post Office postage sticker from Sitka. That makes a coordinate for me, those images allow me to fix very rapidly that time for myself, or anybody else looking at the book, in fact. There's a kind of statement in the very beginning, before anything is done, practically, telling myself what I want to do.

I'm telling myself that this is a book which will be defined by work procedures, which might be common to nearly anyone, and in that spirit, I want it to be not *for* anyone in particular, not even myself. One of the very first ideas I have is, everybody dispersed, and I went to California. I can see a phrase here concerning the address to La Jolla because it is the supremest social terminal. I'm likening it to a moraine, continuous mini-rocks of foreign lithology, foreign lithologies, a usage I picked up that same day from an article in *Nature* on the rock system around the Rio Grande and the Grand Canyon. And one of my purposes for being down there was to do a course in the descent of the Grand Canyon to the Colorado River.

Then, after a while there's this entry, which concerns a section in the book. The sections are called: *Suppertime Down South, Hello La Jolla, Flywheel Programs* and *101: That Great Zero Resting Eternally between Parallels.* While driving through the city on route 101, the *101* section was written with one hand tied to the wheel. This is the section in which I learned to write while driving. Because I didn't want to waste any time. If you live in California you can spend a lot of time on the freeway. And it becomes quite apparent that you'd better learn to do something with that time, besides listening to the radio, or watching the passing landscape, or whatever. It's too much to lose, so certain illegalities must be practiced, simply not to waste time. That was an idea that occurred to me once I had started to *read* while driving. The trick is to learn to write without taking one's eyes off the road. That can be mastered in about five minutes or less, if you're bright and clever. It starts out as a scrawl, but it can be developed, it can get fancy, and it can get—but the point is, it only *needs* to be clear. And you can write a lot while driving. So, I mean, this notation is to remind me to recommend that process to all those who do a lot of driving.

Now on this page, there are a series of attempts and starts to write something. Some of them were later used, some were not: "His arrogance is seriously flawed by its vast emptiness." "Contempt and distrust." "You are not to come within a hundred Italian miles of shore." That was simply an attempt to make use of Italian miles, which I also read that day. That's a unit of measure that's used up, it slipped away from me a little bit, but it has a peculiar use, it might be nautical. But they're still used, Italian miles. I find it very provocative. "Would you mind keeping it down? You're kinda hoggin the atmosphere out there." That, I think, comes as a consequence of a lot of navy jets flying over this housing development where I was staying in La Jolla. And then, this is an example that I don't have to read. Yes, this is really of no consequence at all, it was just a fleeting thought derived from something someone said to me, perhaps, about Lew Welch, one day, down there, "and oh yes, Lew Welch is not dead, he's missing in action." That will never see any use, I mean it's just, there . . . "Easy Oakland, there's a roll over in the hotland." That's *101.* And this is a quote: "The marvelous quality of making everybody feel so terribly at ease," Robert Wagner; If you didn't know a thing, you could read *Chicken Itza* (from *Hello La Jolla,* Wingbow, June, 1978) ; "Toothless from Scurvy," (from my notebooks) .

All right, that's a grid. Then I come to something finished. This comes from a visit to Safeway:

> Poetry is not mostly government product.
> So the work of our non-existent critics is unnecessary
> the grades assigned to meat will do nicely
> Prime
> Choice
> good
> commercial
> utility
> canners
> Environmental carcinogen and large fowl cancer
> Tuesday, 2 March 1976, weather report
> The sky for sure
> is soup de jour.

Here's *101,* and that's another thing I should mention about writing while driving, the product is gonna be low-grade actually. Not always, but much of it is just something to do, it's another way of killing time. Here's one, for instance, something I wouldn't actually *use,* because it's that topical, it's called, and you'll recognize it, it's called *Tight Shoes and Cold Igloos.*

> One mildly electric campaign joke of 1976 possessed a point of interest, namely the amount of euphemism generated by what were originally euphemisms. I discovered the extremest pleasure to step on the devil's neck and yet to enjoy the use of him.

That's *Hello La Jolla.*

101: "He was sidetracked by the molecular structure of bricks at 3:60 p.m., the merest shade before four." And there's a few other things I've yet to do.

QUESTION: You seem to be saying that the random things are, in a way at least, preferable to those consciously organized in a work, that the important thing is the quality of attention at the moment of writing. I was wondering if you would say something about other forces that bring unity to the poem?

ED DORN: I didn't say random, I wouldn't say that. And I wouldn't want to suggest that either. Unity is a psycho-philosophical pressure and has nothing to do with a poem. The instrumentation of language itself is an active audience, with its own ideas and its own content and its own need to make its expression; and I look at the foot as the agency of that, that's correct, and with a nod to that severest of special flaws, "footloose." But that's in no sense random. In fact, I'm only interested in the most careful disposition of words on the page.

I've got an example. If I can find it. Well, maybe I can remember it. It might have been a *Flywheel Program,* I'm not sure. "The question is not, which came first/the chicken or the egg/the question is which came first/journalism or tobacco." So I'm going down the street in Boulder and I see this shop called Smoke and News. *Smoke and News* written on the door. Well now, that's not random. That is extremely strict. It simply verifies what everybody's always known—the answer is the egg. Chickens are late! I find it extremely interesting that it's not random. That the expressions are so crucially true, between yourself and the language, that you get verification all over the place. I'd been writing some tobacco poems, and I was interested to see if I couldn't tease out what there is about tobacco. I looked tobacco up, and so then I got interested in using that form of it: tobaccum. And I was interested in it as a drug, in tobacco as a drug, because we've lost its drug quality and now we're stuck with its habit, which is, by anybody's estimation, bad. And that's too bad, because in this hemisphere it was the drug of introduction. The first hit of tobacco is to the spine and that's all you need, and it represents brilliance and clarity, and it must have had something to do with the pow-wow, the circle, the conference, all that early habit in America to sit down, 'cause that's the first thing people did here you know, they sat in a circle and the Indians got out their tobacco. They were really putting something out there, you know. And it was obviously a drug which goes very well with consideration, and well, for instance, I'm sure some of the troubles we have now with administrations all over the world are because they don't have the use of tobacco that way. What they should do in their offices is just sit in a circle and pass tobacco, that's the pow-wow rite, I think that's its value. This is not esoteric data by any means. That's how the language makes the connections for you if you want to entertain it that way. I don't like randomness at all, I try to drive randomness right up the wall.

Q: What's the justification for the use of the "line" in poetry, the rationale for ending a line somewhere and beginning it somewhere else?

E.D.: With the passing of strick meter, the justification became less and less necessary, and this is a constant and chronic exacerbation about the legitimacy of the line. The only thing we can hope for is that it will just die of old age as a question. I don't feel that it's important in anyway that I can imagine it to be important. Simply because poetic expression now is, well, to put it this way, it's incumbent upon poetic expression to occupy its space in a real way, optically, which is its present confusion with prose. To optically occupy its space, which is different from saying that it's metrically interesting or not. I think that's a false question, and I think it's been a false question for a long time, simply because content and form, those two great mastodons of modern poetry, have been trying to mutually realize each other in modern expression. Anyone can see that the reading is interesting or occluded or sharp or quick or slow or precise or loose or right or wrong, and it's through all those agencies that we say whether a poem is good, bad, or indifferent. And this question of the line has also done a great damage because of its unresolvability. It's given people the false notion that you can't say those things about poems, when, in fact, you can. It's quite possible to say that a poem is a bad poem, and very often without hesitation for quite precise reasons. People don't like to do it, because it's supposed to be an open question because, well, you can't really tell, can you, and you can't really tell, because, well, is it really poetry, and is it really poetry because you can't really say what a line is. See, I mean it's an excuse, actually, that we shouldn't even allow in the door.

Q: There seems to be no difference between what you'd call good prose and poetry. The only difference is the way they're written down.

E.D.: Those kind of hard and fast distinctions between poetry and prose have, not for practical purposes, but for larger, you know, aesthetically formal purposes, disappeared. There are lots of habits of prose and there are lots of habits of poetry. There's a kind of third and median form that nobody much practices with any kind of public insistence, at least, which is called "the prose-poem." It's kind of a very loose thing to say about anything in English, anyway, because it can't actually be proven that there's anything like the prose-poem. And so we sort of allow it to rest between forms, to have the rhythmic extensions of prose, and yet have the compression of poetic language. And it mostly sells both short.

Now, when you write a poem, your mind suspects how much you want to do with it regarding length, and just flat content, violence or mildness of expression, obliqueness of rhetoric, and all of these considerations. And from that follows the line.

Q: I wondered at Olson's idea of breath and line, line length being determined by breath?

E.D.: I never heard that as procedural. I never thought that his discussion of the breath was meant to be taken as a way you could write poetry. I always thought it was meant to suggest to you that you could get involved physically with the poem in a way that, up to that point, hadn't actually been suggested. And since breathing is one of the—I mean, it is part of the central nervous system's maintenance of perception in that sense—it always struck me as a valuable thing to think about, as well, obviously, as to do. But, for anybody who thought that it was meant to *function* in a way that a VW manual will tell you how to set the valves, I just never took it that way. I've never seen any example of a practice that proved to me that it had been derived from that either.

Q: In a lot of your work the line goes all the way back to the left margin, and then, how do you decide where it ends? I know a lot of us probably use some kind of modified Olson in starting a line in the middle of the rest of lines, you know, away from the margin, but where do you end the line, like maybe there's a comma and one word before the next line begins, and it's not arbitrary.

E.D.: I can remember when I first wrote a line [*laughter.*] I don't remember exactly what I thought, but it seems to me fairly probable that I thought, well, so I can do it, but really, how do I know? That question's a background all the time, so obviously if you mean to continue you've got to forge ahead anyway. But nevertheless, it is something when anybody begins and people are always beginning. And it must be quite peculiar to our epoch. I can't imagine it was a problem in the eighteenth century. I mean, you know, there was a little rule then; when the line went that far, it got cut.

So, you know, no problem in that sense. We have a very large purchase on the hyphen of irrationality.

Sources

WITTGENSTEIN, LUDWIG VON, *On Uncertainty* (New York: Harper and Row, 1969), arts. 56, 58, 59, and 61.

Photo by Andrea Craig

Michael McClure

CINNAMON TURQUOISE LEATHER: (A PERSONAL UNIVERSE DECK)

JULY 17, 1976

I'M GOING TO give you a set of rules for making a deck of fifty cards containing one hundred words. This is a complex set of rules. Feel free to ask me questions. They may remind me of something that I'm leaving out.

This is called a *personal universe deck.* It is going to be your personal universe exemplified in one hundred words. James Joyce was supposed to have an English vocabulary of one hundred thousand words. Joyce also spoke a dozen languages. If he had five or ten thousand words in each of those languages, you can imagine the scale of Joyce's vocabulary. A normal active vocabulary may vary from five thousand to twenty thousand words. To pick only one hundred words from your vocabulary to exemplify your personal universe is a challenging process.

To follow this set of rules you will pick words that exemplify your past, your present, and if you can imagine, your future: some of these hundred words will reach into your future and exemplify it also. These hundred words will represent your *personal universe* in the past, present, and future.

The next rule is that the one hundred words must sound good together. It's even better if they sound beautiful together. But, at least, they must sound good together in *any random combination.* As I understand it, someone found out from Edgar Allen Poe that he thought that the most beautiful word in English was "cellar door." The recognition of what sounds good, or beautiful, to you is in your own ears. For instance, anybody would agree that Chaucer sounds good. Say the *Canterbury Tales* aloud:

> Whan that Aprill with his shoures sote
> The droghte of Marche hath perced to the rote,
> And bathed every veyne in swich licour
> of which vertu engendred is the flour;
> Whan Zephirus eek with his sweet breeth
> Inspired hath in every holt and heeth
> The tendre croppes, and the yonge sonne
> Hath in the Ram his halve cours yronne,
> And smale fowles maken melodye,
> That slepen al the night with open yë[1]

There's not disputing the fact that those words sound good in those combinations. Or, if we recite Blake:

> How sweet I roam'd from field to field,
>   and tasted all the summer's pride,
> 'Till I the prince of love beheld,
>   Who in the sunny beams did glide!
>
> He show'd me lilies for my hair,
>   And blushing roses for my brow;
> He led me through his gardens fair,
>   Where all his golden pleasures grow.[2]

We know that sounds good. Or to take something that's not in English, recite this in Spanish:

> Nadie comprendia el perfume
> de la oscura magnolia de tu vientre.[3]

That's the "Gacela of Unforeseen Love" from *The Divan at Tamarit* by Lorca.

What if you randomly say: "Shit, Venezuela, Hamburger"? Sounds terrible? What if you said "Shit, Musk, Velvet"? Or "Shit, Musk"? Or "Velvet, Musk, Shit"? If you say "Shit, Venezuela, Hamburger" it doesn't sound good.

QUESTION: Shit doesn't sound good to me.

MICHAEL MCCLURE: Well, you're going to make up your own list of one hundred words.

Here's the next rule. You must show your good side as well as your bad side. The hundred words can't all come from your angel-food self. You want some of the dark flesh in there too. Some of your negative aspect. Don't use a hundred words to tell the world that you're an angel. Remember the demonic, sinister side of yourself also.

Okay. It's going to be a personal universe, one hundred words from your past, present and future. The words should sound good, or beautiful together, in any *random* combination. A word that sounds bad to your ear by itself may sound beautiful in combination with ninety-nine other words that enable the word to express its beautiful aspects. For instance, when Allen [*Ginsberg*] says "Hamburger, Shit Venezuela," he'll add ninety-seven other words to fill those words out. Then when they combine you'll hear their many facets, and the fricatives and the vowels interacting, and the gentle beauteous parts of the breath that are in their interdependence. That's exactly what *Howl* does, as a matter of fact.

Q: Does the repetition of one word over and over make it sound more beautiful?

M.M.: It might or might not. It depends on the circumstances.

When you're drawing up the·list of a hundred words, if a word comes up obsessively two or three times and you don't notice, if it sneaks in, you may use that word more than once in your hundred words. Possibly its multiple occurrence represents an unconscious, impulsive desire to join the list more than once. You can pay attention to that.

Q: What about words that are synonyms or opposites for each other?

M.M.: If you've got a hundred words to express your past,

present, and future, your good side and your bad side, how many synonyms do you want to use?

Q: Can you make up words?

M.M.: Absolutely; make up one or two for feelings you don't have words for.

Q: Do you want any particular grammatical distribution?

M.M.: The words should be bare of endings. If you want to say *star,* don't say *starry.* If you want to say *stare,* don't say *stared.* If you want to say *tooth,* don't say *toothy.* If you want to say *sparkle* don't say *sparkly.* Don't use endings such as "ings," "ies." Don't use plurals. Reduce words to their most concrete, original, basic grammatical structure. Reduce words to their grammatic concrete base. In this hundred words, all except a few should be absolutely concrete.

Q: What do you mean by concrete?

M.M.: That's a question I'll put off for five minutes.

The one hundred words are going to tend to be nouns. But don't look at them as nouns. View them as basic concrete language. Let's not use grammatical terms to describe a word, because that limits the possibility of the word in this imaginative and experimental context. Mostly they will be basic nouns. Some words will work in other ways. You'll discover that they have adjectival and verbal connotations when you free them. So, no endings. No plurals. We want to use real words. The words are to be concrete.

Eighty of these concrete words will be divided evenly among Sight, Sound, Taste, Touch, Smell. That's sixteen apiece. So, there will be sixteen words of sight, sixteen words of sound, sixteen words of taste, sixteen words of touch, and sixteen of smell.

Here's what would happen if you didn't follow this set of directions. About seventy-five percent of concrete, conscious, verbal information is visual. If you don't follow the rule that divides the words equally among sight, sound, taste, touch, and smell, you'll have seventy or eighty *sight* words in the hundred. That's the *natural, conscious* distribution. The function of dividing the words into five equal units is to achieve the arranged derangement of the senses, of which Rimbaud spoke. By evenly dividing our personal *one hundred word consciousness* over the five senses, we break up our normal *set*. Then, other processes begin to take hold and we operate more fully in new fashions. There are other areas than the conscious ones. You'll see them as you begin this experimental exercise.

So, there will be sixteen sight words, sixteen sound words, sixteen taste words, sixteen touch words, and sixteen smell words. That's eighty of the hundred words.

Next, there will be ten words of movement. They're words describing movement—like *handspring, swim, talk, run, surf, skate*. Notice, no endings. It's not *skating, surfing, swimming, handspringing,* but *surf, swim,* etc.

For this exercise, avoid terms like verb or noun. You'll find out that words aren't verbs or nouns anymore. There's no sense in thinking of them as verbs or nouns when you're making your list. You'll find out right away that they are something else also.

That leaves ten words.

Remember, these words are from past, present, and future. They represent your good side and your bad side.

We'll turn to the concept of concrete, which is puzzling some people. But before that, let's look at how one is going to delve for a hundred words from past, present, and future. You will have to be in a special state—a rapport with yourself. The best way to get this state is to temporarily send away your roommate, your lover, the dog, the cat, the television set—and definitely, absolutely—the record player. You must sit someplace in semidarkness, quite still without persons coming in and out of the room. You must be really alone, able to find a companionability with your past, your present, your future.

You must be able to feel the aura of your past, present, and future around yourself, and feel the weaving of your good and bad and sweet and bitter nature through the aura that you're allowing to exist. The best way I know of to do this is to go to a semidark room without even a cat there.

The cat is not part of your interior personal universe. Nothing should be there except a candle—a little candlelight. If you do this list by candlelight it helps consciousness to expand at the peripheral edges. Just a candle in darkness, or maybe a dim desk lamp, and a pencil and a piece of paper. Let your verbal universe exist around you and then become conscious of it. There will be your whole vocabulary world, and you'll be able to move right through it to make the right choices quite easily.

Q: You write down words as they come to you?

M.M.: That's the intuitive way of doing it. An individual sits down and simply writes out his hundred words. You wouldn't believe how many people absorb the rules and write out sixteen sight, sixteen sound, sixteen taste, sixteen touch, sixteen smell, etc., and have their hundred words immediately. On the other hand, it's common for people to write sixty words immediately and then lengthily sort around for the last forty. I've also seen people write two or three hundred words and then cut the list to a hundred.

Okay, the last ten words. One or two will be parts of the body. Parts of the body that are really significant to your personal universe. *That puts the chips right on the table!*

Q: Does this have to be *your* body?

M.M.: No, it doesn't have to be your body. It could be somebody else's. Your mother's, your lover's.

Also, in this last ten words will be names of heroines or heroes. And also, places in the universe. Plus invented words. And times of the night and day. Also, symbolic signs like astrological signs. Don't forget totemic animals. And birds and plants. You must also save one word for the *abstraction* that has the most significance to you. Could your abstraction be Patriotism? Thriftiness? Prayer? Industry?

That is the rule for ten final words. Use them for parts of the body, names of heroes and heroines, places in the universe, invented words, times of night and day, symbolic signs, totemic animals, birds and plants, and one abstraction.

What is the most significant abstraction in your life? You

shouldn't brood on it; you should possibly take the first answer that comes into your head.

Last thoughts on the deck are: avoid hyphenated words if you can. Use them when you need to. Remember, the one hundred words have to sound good, or beautiful, together in any random combination.

I'm going to pretend that I'm all by myself in a dark room with a candle. I've just put the cat out, turned the record player off, and I'm remembering a list of rules Michael McClure gave me at a lecture. I've got a pencil and a piece of paper. My personal way to do it is by free association. I'll remember past, present, future, good and bad sides, sight, sound, taste, touch, smell, and that the words must sound good in any combination. Well, I've always liked roses. ROSES! Oh, it's supposed to be singular! Okay, ROSE! Let's see, is that a sight? A smell? A taste? It could be, in the case of a rose. This is one of the trickiest words you run into. Is it a verb? It *rose* up in front of me. It's probably either sight or smell. How many persons see a rose when you say *rose?* How many smell a *rose?* In my case it's *sight.* I saw it. Sometimes I smell it, but this time I see it. So, a *sight* word. Now I'm going to free associate. THUNDER! A childhood word, Kansas, thunderstorms, THUNDER! Then SWIM comes right out. Now I *know* what THUNDER is, that's sound. See, it's really up to you, isn't it? TURQUOISE. Strangely, TURQUOISE is a touch for me. TURQUOISE has a tactile sensation. I like to touch turquoises.

Q: When you free associate, do you keep all the other words in mind at the same time to see how they sound together?

M.M.: That's an important point. When you get some words down, you have to keep checking them to see if they're going well together.

Let me free associate a couple of smell words. By the way, smell is *really* tough to get words for. Sixteen good smell words? Remember spices when you're doing it. Often spices out of your childhood, or out of your future, have particular strength. CINNAMON . . . MUSK . . . a perfume.

I'll check randomly for their sound quality . . . TURQUOISE THUNDER MUSK ROSE . . . ROSE THUNDER LEATHER TURQUOISE . . . CINNAMON TURQUOISE MUSK SWIM LEATHER . . . THUNDER ROSE TURQUOISE MUSK. I like them all. Now let's say for a fantasy that I'm a hamburger addict. For the last twenty-seven years the only thing I've eaten is hamburgers. I have a couple for breakfast, and since that's kind of heavy I have one for lunch, and then I get hungry around dinnertime and have three hamburgers for dinner. Once in awhile at midnight I go out to McDonald's and have a hamburger. That's the only thing I eat. It doesn't seem fair to me to pick out a hundred words that are significant in my past, present, and future, and leave out hamburger. The candle is twitching and flickering and I'm looking at it and saying, "HAMBURGER, HAMBURGER, HAMBURGER." I don't want to say hamburger. I just had the horrible thought that hamburger isn't going to sound right with TURQUOISE and MUSK. My conscience is hot on my heels. HAMBURGER! I exclaim! ROSE HAMBURGER THUNDER. HAMBURGER has got to go with all of them! LEATHER HAMBURGER MUSK ROSE . . . CINNAMON HAMBURGER . . . That sounds good! But LEATHER CINNAMON HAMBURGER? No! This puts me in a dilemma! I want the list to be honest. How about GROUND BEEF LEATHER? ROSE GROUND BEEF?

I determine that hamburger doesn't work in my list. But it remains an enigma because it's too significant to leave out. The fellow in the back suggests MEAT. So, MEAT is a constituent of a hamburger. What are the other constituents? MEAT is a category and I'd rather be more specific. So BEEF might be better. BREAD? BUN? ONION? MUSTARD? Could it be KETCHUP, MUSTARD, GREASE, PICKLE? If HAMBURGER doesn't work, I'm going to have to go after the essential quality. I've tried BURGER, it doesn't work either. I'm going to break HAM-

BURGER down into its constituents. I'm a purist at heart. I love them for the BEEF and the BREAD—or the MEAT and the BREAD. I like the sound of MEAT. I'm going to get rid of HAMBURGER. I found the word. It's meat. Maybe it's BREAD too.

MEAT. I wonder what category that goes into? That's a taste word. BREAD? Is that a *touch* or a *taste?* Now let's go on. I love birds. BIRD! But I don't want categories. I'm going to have to say what kind of bird. A toucan, a sparrow, a falcon, a parrot, a hawk. I was thinking of a FALCON. I think that's going to sound good with the other words. I'm going to test this again. FALCON TURQUOISE LEATHER ROSE. . . . I know a lot about falcons. It sounds good, too. I love plants. I love trees. TREE! That's a good one, but that too is a category. I was seeing a REDWOOD. It could have been an oak or a maple. I come from San Francisco, so when I think of trees I either think of oaks on the hills or redwoods. The REDWOOD is my tree. That's a sight word. Don't say trees, don't say animal, don't say bird, don't say flower, say ROSE, say REDWOOD, say AIRDALE, say TOUCAN, say FALCON.

Q: If you have a word that's applicable to past, present and future—like write—how do you assign it?

M.M.: You don't have to assign words to past, present and future. Make sure you're using all the areas. Sometimes it's a little harder to see into the future than other times. If you get a few from the future then you're doing well. Most of them will come out of the past or present, and there's no need to assign them. That rule is to remind you to create a structure that you're reaching through for the words. You'll find that when you put yourself in a rapport, it's quite easy to find the state. If you just move into the state and remember past, present, and future, then you're not just reaching through shapelessness. Nobody's ever had any trouble doing this. You'll find the area.

Now I write RAPHAEL. That's right out of the unconscious. RAPHAEL is a hero. I know little regarding Raphael except his paintings, and I love them. When I become "arrangedly disarranged" in my senses, Raphael always comes out.

Q: Have you accounted for both the good and bad sides of your personality?

M.M.: No. I haven't gotten to that yet.

While showing some people how to do this, I found out one of the ways my consciousness works. I had a list much like this one. It had the word CURRY. I am very fond of curries. We eat curries often. They're almost a work of art. A beautiful curry is a wonderful thing. It's a kind of disappearing sculpture. It's a sculpture that you eat; the finely cut meat and the elegant combination of many spices. The combining and cooking of curry spices is a complex thing. CURRY sounds good, too, to the ear. CURRY MUSK LEATHER ROSE . . .

Around my house there are many tartans. You know, those Scottish capes with the plaids representing the clans. We've got a lot of those around because they're lovely, because they look great in the house, and because I love the feel of mohair. I love those colors and the Hibernian, vibrant combinations of them. One day, making a list, I was free associating and got CURRY. The next word was TARTAN. TARTAN ROSE CURRY MUSK THUNDER LEATHER FALCON. . . . I saw why TARTAN came after CURRY; this is an example of "synesthesia." I went from CURRY to TARTAN. *(Who is the most synethesiac poet? Apollinaire? Mallarme? Keats? Synesthesia is the experience in one sense modality of an entirely different sense. It is a transfer of sense modalities. For instance: blue taste of coffee, the chocolate sound of the music, or the dark brown sound of Brahms. Baudelaire wrote of a "blue" perfume.)*

I see the odor of curries in a synesthesiac way. When one is fixing a curry and is right over the spices, when one has them in his hands and is powdering or crumbling them, there can be a vision in the mind's eye. You have to have tumeric and cumin—those are the two basic spices.

I was seeing the tumeric—which is a dark yellowish

spice—in my mind's eye drifting through the room. Tumeric is very heavy, the basic spice in curry. The tumeric gives the yellow color and a high register taste. Also, I was seeing the cumin making wave patterns alongside the tumeric pattern.

I was seeing the coriander as quite vital, making a kind of slash in the design. Then the lovely cinnamon comes in. The cinnamon has a whole tonality, and goes through it like that—like a pattern of checks. The cayenne, or red pepper, gives a little accent to the whole thing, like this—like a dot and a bar. I realized I was seeing the CURRY as a TARTAN in my consciousness. I was seeing curry as a tartan floating through the air in a plaid pattern. On the chairs in the room were Scottish tartan capes making a ripple pattern where they were draped. Tartan and curry were melting together. I free associated from CURRY to TARTAN.

The first deck I saw was made up by a seven-year-old girl. Her father and a friend of his printed it in a small edition to give away as presents. I began to see that it had many more possibilities and more dimensions. I created this set of rules.

Q: Is this deck itself comprised of a series of poems? Do you use them as seeds for poems?

M.M.: I don't use them as seeds for poems and I don't consider the deck to be a poem. Decks are word sculptures. I consider them to be a way of creating spontaneous, subjective, stochastic imagery reflecting the personal self. It is better not to think of this as poetry. Remove yourself from that aspect of it. This needs alchemical, transformational possibilities. If you get into literary areas it's not going to take you anywhere. Think of it as an alchemic word experiment, or as word sculpture.

There are many things that can be done with this deck. You'll know if you made the deck right. If it is done correctly it will get you a little high. It will reflect back your interior and subjective reality models in unusual combinations. You get a little spirit-life from it.

A definition: *Stochastic* means that one has limited the number of chance possibilities, or that one is drawing randomly from a *limited* number of possibilities. In other words, you'll have a hundred possibilities with the deck. You'll draw from them in random combinations. That's stochastic—as compared to totally random or pure chance. Stochastic is a controlled chance.

Stay concrete. Stay with things you can see, hear, taste, touch, and smell. If you're doubtful about specific word choices, remember that you have many thousands of other words in your vocabulary. If you're doubtful about whether it's an abstraction or if it is concrete, then opt for one that's concrete.

Be as romantic as you want, but don't mechanically use romantic things. Use REDWOOD, QUARTZ, MOSS, WAVES, OCEAN, CINNAMON, ENVY, SWIM . . .

Q: Say more about distribution and choice of category.

M.M.: Well, I just chose five senses. As you know, we have twenty-seven senses rather than five. It's not that we're told by mystics that we have twenty-seven senses. We're told that we have twenty-seven senses by scientists. We have organs of interior affective perception. Our sense of taste may be comprised of several chemical tastes. We have kinesthetic senses. We have conscious and non-conscious senses. In this deck we're using the five traditional senses because they're the ones we deal with best in language. I once used six categories of sense. The sixth category was *interior affective perception* because it took into account about twenty senses. But if one picks concretely from Sight, Sound, Taste, Touch, and Smell, one gets the interior, affective perceptions anyway.

Stay away from troublesome speculations. Forget philosophy and forget poetry. Give yourself over to the rules. They're simple if you don't confuse them. It's about you.

Here's what to do with the words. First you need three-by-five cards. You'll need fifty, and you may as well have a few extra. Put them in a stack next to your piece of paper with the hundred words on it. You should have a dark pen with a big tip to write the words in block capitals when you transfer them to the cards. That will make the cards easier to use. Go to your list and cross off a word. ROSE. Then write ROSE on the top center of the card in big, clear block capitals. Then, at random, go to the list and take another word. Look, that was MOON that time. Write it in block capitals at the other end. Okay, then you take another card. Go over the list at random and cross off TURQUOISE, and cross off THUNDER. You know how the heads of the king and queen are on a deck of playing cards? One head is up this way and the other head is up that way. That's the way you want the words. Pretty soon you have a piece of paper with a hundred words crossed off, and you have fifty three-by-five cards with the hundred words on them. You do it randomly so that you take combining out of your conscious control. You'll find that method has many more dimensions.

There are lots of things you can do with the cards: play games with them, make conversations with them, tell jokes with them, make poems with them.

'Till then—ROSE APPLE INK LIGHT!

Sources

BLAKE, WILLIAM, "Poetical Sketches (1783), Song." From *The Poetry and Prose of William Blake,* eds. David V. Erdman and Harold Bloom. Copyright 1965 by David V. Erdman and Harold Bloom. Reprinted by permission of Doubleday & Company, Inc.

CHAUCER, GEOFFREY, from "General Prologue to *The Canterbury Tales.*" Reprinted from *The Works of Geoffrey Chaucer* by F.N. Robinson. Copyright ©1933, 1957, renewed 1961. Used by permission of the publisher, Houghton Mifflin Co.

LORCA, GARCIA, "Gacela of Unforeseen Love," from *The Divan at Tamarit, Obras Completas* (Madrid: Aguilar Press).

Photo by Roger Paige/San Francisco Arts Commission

Ron Padgett

STOICALLY BEDAZZLED

AUGUST 3, 1975

I WAS INVITED to do a workshop, then when I got here they said, your "lecture." Well, I'm not going to do a lecture. But what I'd like to do is—everybody has some paper and stuff, right? Great, give me all your paper and pencils. No, just kidding, but I'd like to do some writing with you and I didn't bring any paper myself. Anyway, here's the idea. (Good to get chalk, hold it in your hand, move it around in the air) . I'm used to teaching, like for a living I teach poetry writing to kids like in the third, fourth grade, you know. So if you find me talking down at you . . . [*laughter*]. Most of my students are like this tall [*indicates three feet high*], they pull on my leg to get my attention. So I'm not used to being with like, grown-up people [*laughter*].

So, listen, this is about poetry writing, and that's really all I'm gonna say. I was thinking recently that in a sense there are two kinds of poetry. Anytime you say "there's two kinds of," it's wrong, always. As in: there are two kinds of walnuts, two kinds of people—that's ridiculous, of course. But bear with the idea anyway. OK, there are two kinds of poetry. Now, one kind is preconceived, you know, that's where the writer will say, "I have an idea," like he's in love with a woman or he's in love with a goat, in love with something.

Or let's say he feels unhappy: usually a lot of poetry comes out of being unhappy, you know like, my stomach hurts, or I'm going to die tomorrow, or my mother hates me, something like that. In this case the poet has a preconceived message he wants to convey. He takes this message and makes a poem which will embody it. Recently this kind of poetry has been kind of dry; at its best, it's referred to as "well-crafted verse." Poets such as Richard Wilbur write that way, sometimes beautifully. They all have an idea, this beautiful structure, and will express this idea. But there's very little excitement, for me, in that kind of writing. It's like *work,* hard work, and then you have to cover up the work, so people don't know how hard you sweated to make this thing. So, that's one kind of poetry.

Let me give you an analogy: it's like you're gonna go on vacation this summer, right? You say, well, two months. I'll need X thousand dollars. Where will we go? So you get a map, you plot it out. First day we'll drive to here and we'll stay overnight, we'll stay, you know, at the Holiday Inn. Next day we'll go here, here, then we'll stay for three days and fish, you know, all very thought-out and planned carefully. 'Cause you have to be back on a certain date, and there are little variations along the way, but basically you stick to this plan. Now that's kind of like this one kind of poetry I've been talking about, where you plan out a thing and you do it, as exactly as you can. It's kind of dull, actually, but it's admirable in its way, too.

Now there's another kind, where you get in the car with a thousand bucks, and you just start driving down the street and you don't have any idea where you're going to go. You come to the corner and you take a left, right, or straight ahead, unless you want to go backwards, which is a possibility, too. It's much more interesting, it's more exciting. Of course you can end up running out of gas in the middle of the desert—it involves all sorts of dangers. But it's wonderful to be able to go to the typewriter at any given moment; you can wake up in your sleep and just start writing. And in fact that's really thrilling. I mean, lots of times you write absolute baloney that way, real garbage. But it's usually more fun, and that's the kind of poetry I prefer writing. But we're not going to do any of that today.

I'm going to give you some writing things to do, and I want to do them too. They're a little bit more like the second kind I'm talking about. You may have done some of this, and if you want to interrupt me, please do, or if you want to ask me anything, or if it's boring, please butt in. I don't know what you've done, anyhow, I just came from New York and don't know what's going on.

Anyway, you guys know what acrostics are? Acrostics—who doesn't know? Oh good: one. This brainy bunch is smarter than me. OK, you take any word or sentence, "Naropa," say. Now, usually you write the word, N-A-R-O-P-A, like that, left to right, horizontally. I always get "horizontal" and "vertical" confused, I never did really learn those. It's like "pineapple" and "grapefruit," I always get them confused. Anyway, NAROPA. So usually, you write like that, horizontally, but in an acrostic, you write it down, vertically, like that. Now there is the letter N, wonderful letter N, the fourteenth letter of the alphabet. Someone tell me any word starting with N, any word at all. I have nothing up this sleeve, I have nothing up—no, *any* word at all, come on! Anything starting with N. Necrophilia, any other idea? Yeah, No. Any others? Now. Noodle. Nibble. Neuter. OK, which one of these should we use? Nehru. You like Necrophilia? OK. How about, noodle, nibble. Nibble is nice. OK, nibble. Now, Nibble. Should we make that a verb, like a thing happening—Nibble? OK. Nibbles, you like that. OK, next any word starting with A. "Always," OK. Now, Nibbles Always. Hmm, who's doing the nibbling, or what's doing the nibbling, you have any idea, think about nibbles and something nibbling. Rats? OK. Well, it would have to be Rat [*pointing to third letter in "Naropa"*] Right? Rabbit? Necrophilia? [*Laughter*]—Necrophilia and Rats, no, it doesn't work. Make it complete. You could say, The Rabbit Nibbles Always. All right, what starts with R, any word—Rhubarb? The Rhubarb, because it—Opens? Thank you. It opens, what? Any word—Pie? Pie in the sky?—at Once, OK. Now I haven't been following it, so—The Rabbit Nibbles Always the Rhubarb Because It Opens Pie in the Sky at Once. That's strange. It's nice that this rabbit would nibble on the rhubarb, and this pie in the sky is nice, you know, it could mean a lot of things, but if you see a big pie floating in the sky, opening up, a marvelous rabbit. . . . Oh, I like that. Anyway, so we turned the word Naropa on its side, and out came this rabbit, jumping out, eating this rhubarb, causing a mysterious thing to happen in the sky. Now, this is called an "across-tic." One kid said it should be called "down-ics."

This is a Victorian parlor game, by the way, it's not some modern poetry thing, it's just this old Victorian game. Also in the nineteenth century, people would send "secret" messages to each other this way. They would write a message this way, vertically, like I Love You, and then they would fill it in with sentences and stuff, the way we just did, and they would give the note to a person who could read down and get the message. Mom and Dad wouldn't know!

Anyway, listen, let's try one more, OK? Somebody suggest another down word, it could be anything. Asphyxiation? Wonderful. Asphyxiation, however, [*spells it on board*] is that right? Looks weird going up and down. Looks right enough, it doesn't matter anyway. OK, A, anything with A. Apple. Uh, I'm gonna, can I, I'm gonna cheat. "My Adam's"—is there an apostrophe in there? I'm in this school so I'm scared of misspelling things. OK, my Adam's Apple, Stuck? Stuck, say got stuck, got Stuck with Peanut Butter. However, Your Xylophone Interprets—A is next, Ancient, Texts, Your Xylophone Interprets Ancient Texts, in Our Nose? OK. Oh, that's nice, Adam's Apple and Nose, too, that's progress. My Adam's Apple Got Stuck with Peanut Butter, However, Your Xylophone Interprets Ancient Texts in Our Nose. OK, now I want everyone in here to write a fifty page essay on that [*laughter*]. To be published by Grove Press, Allen Ginsberg will take care of everything.

Anyway, it's very interesting. Anybody have any idea what it means?

QUESTION: It could be teeth in an upward movement.

RON PADGETT: What? Teeth in an awkward movement?

Q: Upward movement.

R.P.: Upward movement, teeth in an upward movement.

Q: Dental work.

R.P.: Oh yeah, teeth and xylophone, yeah. Right. Oh yeah. I like the idea of peanut butter and ancient texts, too.

ALLEN GINSBERG: Xylophonic teeth.

R.P.: Yeah, right, it's like in Bugs Bunny. Beautiful, I like that. Anyway, now I'd like everybody to pick any word you want, *any* word, and write it vertically like that, and then fill it in, with as many words as you want, out here to the right. The first thing that pops into your mind. And you can put words on this (left) side, too, to make sentences, don't worry about being poetical or anything, just the first thing that pops into your mind, you know, it doesn't have to make any sense. . .

Q: Can it be two words instead of one, like Barn Door?

R.P.: Sure, yeah, fine, as many words as you want, you decide. It's good to start with a word that has about six or eight or ten letters, use your own name if you want.

OK, I'm going to read all this aloud now. Here we go, "Dill Pickles Underwent Massive B-invasions while Atilla the Hun Impishly Threw Elephants under the Restaurant Door." The word Dumb Waiter. Weird. Here's the next one. "Persons Who Owed Lots of Money Yesterday Got Carried Away on the Mississippi's Yule Tide Scream, Down River," . . . Yule Tide Scream Down River. Gee, I hope that doesn't happen to me. Oh, the word was Polygamy. Alimony is more like it. Anyway, here's the next one, on the same paper. "Necromancy Edits Out Lots of Italics from the Hellenic Ideographs of Crete." That was from the word Neolithic. "Eggplant Is Always Soft Cooked". . . . I carry you from the divine to the ridiculous in one easy step—anyway, "Eggplant Is Always Soft Cooked, The Extremes of Romance Sing under National

Detente, Ask Your Friend." The Extremes of Romance Sing under National Detente, Ask Your Friend. Oh, the word—the word was Easter Sunday. "The Bumble Bee Opens His Uppermost Laboratory Where He Dances Every Night Round Some Clamshells with the Dancing Olives. A Labrador Retriever and Olive Oil." That word was Boulder, Colo. "How Simply the Hamburger Omitted Washing Our Earthly Repast." From the word Shower. "Following Others, Remained Only a Notion in the Mind of Carlos, 'Animated Truth Implies Open Knowledge,' she said." Did he teach here, this Carlos? [*Laughter.*] Anyway, that word is Fornication. "Playing Kino Inherits Tarred Use of Chocolate Herbs and Engine Noises." That's from Kitchen. "Towards Vast Accountable Mountains We Plied, Irredeemably, Recklessly, Empurpled by Sky." It's beautiful. That's from Vampire. "The Trombones Ended All Newtonian Notions of Isolated Sisters. Seventeen Harlots Opened on an Early Sunset." And that's from Tennis and Shoes. Beautiful, isn't it? Nice that these trombones just sort of destroyed some old-fashioned notion of the way the universe worked. "Saturn Fish Ride the Trolley Cars over Worth for Anteaters and Wobbly Brown Empirin Pills, Rolled under Red Yo-yos." That'd make a nice Surrealist painting, wouldn't it? The word was Strawberry. "Colorado Marching Band, Avocados Understand Meager Beaver, Can Expand Elephant Eggplant Jar in Can Laugh Illusion." That came from Camel. A very Arabic work, if I ever saw one. "The Bouncing Beyond Runners of Kicked Down the Sky Energizes the Feet of Naked Dancers of Rose Petal under Blue Moon." That's beautiful, like a rough translation from the Japanese. It has that nice fractured English.

Sometimes I feel I'm getting sort of stultified in the way I'm writing, you know, and I start to feel like a parody of myself. Sometimes I write things pretending I'm from a foreign country, and that I know English just very little, and badly speak it, you know. I pretend I'm from Africa, a pygmy or something, and I've just come to New York and I've been there only six months, but I know a little English.

It's very interesting to pretend you're from a foreign country and writing in very bad English, as bad as possible. You get to throw the words away and not worry about it.

Anyway, "The Bouncing Beyond Runners Have Kicked down the Sky Energizes the View of Naked Dancers of Rose Petal under Blue Moon. Oh, Broken Drum" "For Billiard Players, the Interview Glides Smoothly across Melting Fields of Ice, Trickling into Hoboken." Beautiful, that interview gliding smoothly across melting fields of ice, trickling into Hoboken. Big Smith. The next one: "Six Puppies Ran Urine down Pipes Encrusted with Night-time Invalids Alive with Lust."

Q: That's obviously a New York poet.

R.P.: Oh no, it's more like Charles Bukowski as a veterinarian. That was from Prudential. "Bellowing with Umbrage, the Locker Room Loser Forgot Himself in a Rage of Facial Gargoyles." Oh wow, a rage of facial gargoyles, wow, that's good, that's from Bullfrog. There're some scary bullfrogs in a movie up here called *Tales from Winnie the Pooh,* showing down at the Flatirons Theater. Those bullfrogs are really like the rage gargoyles, or something. "Since the Order of Nobility Was Open to Religious Integrity, Tomcats are Cousins to Frozen Yaks." That's from Sonority. "A Man, While Walking, Laid Down His Basket of Eggs, Right next to the Telephone Booth." That's from Albert. "Sarah Answered, Not Talking, Only Laughing Intensely." That's from a person's name. "Platinum Blonde Opens Her Purse, Craning on Five-Inch Heels to Reach a Glance at Her Nose." That's pretty, that's very pretty. That's from Popcorn. I like that. "Aberrative Urgencies Roar Overtime, Rent Attacking Silence. Never Comprehended Absolutely Reactionary Know-nothingism at the End of the World, Telepathically, Injured My Back, Slipping on Ice, Breaking My Broken Leg, Meant Nothing to Me and Nothing to You, or Thou Either." "Stop Making Mashed Potatoes, All the Arrow Rude Robots Will Relax with the Orangutan While They're Woozy." That's from the little word Sparrow. "The Oxen Rotate Ingeniously with Open Lestragonian Energy."

Wow. What's Lestragonian, I've forgotten, is that from Swift? Oh good, I'm so glad I'm right. "The Incredible Mysteries of the Prow of the Boat Exclude References to My Face except in Closeted Times." That's from the word Imperfect. "The Electric Xerox, at Altamont Makes My Intestines Never Eliminate." "The electric xerox at Altamont," that's beautiful sounding, isn't it? "Precipices Cracking on Animalistic Notions, Delivering Sights the Colored Eagle Mountain Blessing Ordinary to Sage. Never Interrupting Underground Movement of Bedrock." That's from Pandemonium. Some of them are very syntactical and sort of make-sense-ish, and others just sort of spew out crazy. I like those kind too.

"Ostriches, Whose Plumes Allocate Lonesome Etrangers (the French word, foreigners) Seldom If Ever Create Electric Noises Together." That's from Opalescence. "Great Topaz, Every Switch Rolls Away When Will, the Secretary, Daydreams. Solid in Forehead Jungle, Put Lil in Vinegar. Pick Her Out with Your Entrance Fee, Wring Her Eyes with Soup. Free Her Desk. Out on the Amazon Racetrack, Help Her Down." Great Advice. Let's see, that was the person's name. Wait, the first one is, but then one is Flippers. That's somebody's name, oh that's right, I'm sorry, it says "Gerald Flippers Ford." Be great if Flipper became Secretary of State, you know that dolphin on TV. Wouldn't it be great to have an animal as Secretary of State. "So Once Again, Silox, Here We Are, Confronted, Intrinsically Muddled, Stoically Bedazzled, Tapping into Conspicuous Attention, Talents, Visions, Inavoidably Oppressed by Neon." That was Sophistication. "The Fairly Intricate Rhyme Does Major Apostasis on Most Enumerated Nit-picking Tyrolean." "Salvation of Country Includes Systematical Selling of Religious Shanti." [*Laughter.*] "Ants Gather Notions of Other Streams When Tracks of Illumination Compare. Working Hastens Invention of Sour Truths Laid on Us since Ever." And on the other side it says, "Meet Me at Six"—no, just kidding, here's the last one: "Before After Starts Ellipsis, Manipulate Easter Notions Transparently, Parenthetically, Resonating Eggs

Solder Truisms to the Alimentary Reticular Tongue." [*Laughter.*] That's nice, though, that's beautiful, actually. Parenthetically Resonating Eggs Solder Truisms to the Alimentary Reticular Tongue. And that was from Basement Prestart? Anyway, those are acrostics. I think it comes from a Greek word meaning to put things together, to weave them together, to stitch.

Anyway, OK, that's one kind of weird working that I like to do, and I do this sometimes just to pass the time. Sometimes I do things like this, instead of *always* sitting down to write "seriously," saying, this is Poetry, you know, I'm like God, you know, I might die tomorrow. I find that puts a real cramp on my feelings and my contact with the things I want to be in contact with. Where, by doing things like this that are silly and ridiculous, and fun and weird, and sometimes nonsensical and meaningless, I find that that kind of makes me feel happy, that's what it does, it makes me happy in a way about writing, about words, though not happy about life, particularly. But it gives me an attitude towards words that makes me feel good, you know, that I can do pretty much anything I want. I like that feeling.

I'd like to try another thing now, which is similar to acrostics. What I'd like you to do is take a piece of paper and fold it in half like this. Fold across the middle. On the top half of this piece of paper above the fold, write any question you want, as long as it begins with the word "why." And on the bottom half below the fold, I want you to begin a given answer, beginning with "because." Now, my question is OK: why was I named Gilbert? Why does the sun rise in the morning? Why do I have two eyes? Why does my grandmother speak Chinese? Anything. It can either be a true question you're genuinely asking or it can be a made-up question that you don't really give a fuck about anyway. On the bottom half, give an answer. Now—there are questions you can ask, the answer for which you won't know, of course, right? Just so you give an answer that sounds plausible. Don't worry about it, it's not a test or anything. So do it as quickly as you can, will you. Some people are real fast and some people like to think more. [*Pause for writing.*] You know, painters and sculptors get to play with their toys. The bad thing about being a writer is you don't get many toys. You use paper. Pen. Typewriter. I tear each page along its fold, put the "why" questions in one stack and the "because" answers in another stack. OK, now, I'm going to shuffle these piles up separately. I'm going to read them out loud, read them aloud, out loud, I'm gonna read them aloud in a totally new order. In other words your "why" will now have somebody else's "because" as an answer. And your "because" will find another "why" question to go with. I'm reading them back at random. Sometimes this works really well, and sometimes it's a big flop. OK.

"Why don't the Cleveland Indians ever win the World Series?" "Because I can't see past my own erotic rumblings." "Why do monkey women chase me in the morning?" [*Doesn't even need an answer.*] "Because I beckoned to the 'highers' too hard with hard liquor." Gee, I wish I knew about that. Sounds good with those monkey women. "Why do people paint bright green olive puke walls?" "Because they know it is August." I'm sure that wall is very much like August, ugh. "Why do monarch butterflies migrate to the hospitable blue seas?" "Because the chairs in the room are grey." A very good reason. "Why have we been and what next and failing that who is the alternative?" "Because there are two pianos in this room." "Why do the elliptical shadows of my car wheels emulate old men washing their socks?" "Because the men in charge were color blind." "Why doesn't Debbie write me?" "Because the moon never shines on a dilapidated pistachio." "Why are the birds and the bees the only ones that have any fun?" "Because they caught her eye at a sale on Sunday and they wanted the sky and reminded her of the sea, and they were marked down twenty-five percent." Very funny to talk about love, and then things marked down twenty-five percent in the same breath. Usually when people are writing, they don't change their tone so quickly. They stay in one tone the whole time, because that's what's expected of people, I guess. "Why do monkeys throw crayons at stars?" Beautiful idea. "Because poets don't stand on their tongues." Give it a try. Can't do it. "Why did the men come this morning and chop the oak tree down?" "Because where they have the pitching they don't have the hitting, and when they have the hitting, everyone makes errors." That's true. A stumbling baseball team is exactly like an idiot with an axe chopping down a lot of trees for no reason. Both pointless. "Why sit here under fluorescent silly cranky ladies sore throat yearning for sun, thirsty and have to make a phone call?" "Because it's summertime." That's nice, that it starts out very cranky and angry, and then it's nice at the end. "Why do people expect me to create an ego-limiting style beyond which I must not step, for fear of ceasing to be comprehensible?" "Because she had outlived her shade on the parking lot pavement." "Why is red a color and not the time of day?" "Because of the nature of the question." "Why does snow lie upon the red rocks, waiting for winter's return?" "Because they are tired of seeing only white twinkles." Beautiful. Beautiful that the snow would lie on a rock waiting for winter, it gets so tired of looking at the white twinkles, beautiful, like by those lakes up there, Mitchell Lake, those patches of snow. "Why are there eight women for one man in the city of Vancouver, British Columbia?" "Because red red rose, because blue, because bubble, because thus is thus and ever more so." That was a census taker's nightmare. "Why is it that Naropa has been involved in overcharging student housing?" "Because seals' shins are sweet when rubbed with STP." We have complaint forms over here. "Why am I sitting here?" "Because quite simply, they need the money." [*Laughter galore.*] Are we gonna be kicked out? "Why does it say No Smoking above the green blackboard of the ground floor lecture hall of the Sacred Heart Elementary School, which is inhabited for the summer by a Buddhist university?" "Because piranhas gag on finger fish." That's why it says No Smoking. "Why is there no God in the universe?" "Because there's nothing else to do." "Why so much cost asparagus shoes?" "Because she didn't get enough sleep." "Why is

Anne Waldman yawning?" "Because of the stale scent of licorice that permeates my every pore and putrifies at dawn." "Why do the alligators migrate up tree trunks when the Amazon is awash with chimpanzee fur?" "Because you asked that question." "Why do the archbishops gargle with rain water when ballons pop in the park?" "Because it takes all your cabbage." "Why did Hitler love the Flatirons?" Oh, this is beautiful, actually. "Because the heat of the fields makes them thirst a great deal." "Why am I afraid of flies?" "Because obviously the sun hasn't the answer to give, unless you need the warmth." Didn't work. "Why are boys and girls gods?" "Because they can iron the shirts of an entire army." Wonderful. "Why believe in every drop of rain that falls?" "Because we all begin to learn after we leave what we knew." Hmm. Here's a mammoth answer, unbelievable. "Why does sugar cane grow most heartily where those who tend it drink rum?" "Because people don't like reading what they don't understand already. Any statement must contain at least a pretense of meaning. If you put two meaningless statements together, allowing the reader the option of creating his own meaning, or allowing the words to create their own meaning out of chaos, disharmony, and resolution, the reader will not read it, too much work will be required of him." Beautiful, I mean the answer is such a commentary on this project. "Why was Abigail Van Buren allergic?" "Because rooms are handy, and Ron, the teacher, has me enthralled." Who wrote *that*? "Why do I put so much faith in you not doing what I want you to do?" "Because life seems to be the only alternative to eternity." "Why does my liver hurt?" "Because if nobody had fallen through, there wouldn't be a grate in your head." It's pitiful, your liver hurts, there's a grate, someone falling through your body. It's curious, beautiful. "Why does Anne have blue shoes?" "Because children have shorter attention spans." "Why did the jackal talk to the star?" "Because your smile misses your face."

Now, someone told me there's a Chair of Crazy Wisdom, or something like that at this school? A lot of this sort of operation has something in common with what I would imagine that Chair to be. Some of it is sheer idiocy. You notice how some of them you did respond to and some of them you didn't, instinctively. Some seemed "right," and others seemed not quite right. And it's not the problem of either piece, you know: you could have a terrific why question, and a terrific because answer, but when you put them together, there's not a kind of "electricity" between them. You can take a so-so question and a so-so answer and put them together, and sometimes they will be just dynamite. So the ones that didn't work, it wasn't necessarily the fault of the two pieces, it was probably the fault of the arrangement. And, naturally, when you're doing this kind of thing, you can rearrange the pieces.

I used to do a thing and it taught me a lot, I think. I used to write a lot of poems because I was in love with the idea of writing poetry. So I used to write four or five poems a day, at least, for about two years, and they were almost all horrible. But they seemed great at the time, and they were fun, but I finally realized that I was writing a lot of stuff that wasn't very good. So what I would do is take a bad poem. I'd take the first line, you know how a poem usually starts out in a way a poem usually starts, you know, it would be like the start of a sentence, usually. I mean, usually poems don't start in the middle of a sentence. Just like people don't walk up to you and say, "television set, and the next thing I knew"—they say, "I bought a new television set." So, usually, if you start a poem, it will sound like it started. Likewise, when it ends, it usually sounds like it's ending. You should watch out for that, because it's very corny when you get to the end of the poem and make it end in a "big" way. So anyway, what I would do is type the first line on a new piece of paper, type the *last* line as second line, the former second line would become new line three, the old penultimate line would become new line four, and so on. Now, when you look at it and read it, it'll give you a totally new point of view as to what are some new possibilities, of the, say, ninety words there. As they stand they're not very good. So how can I redo them? I would type it up like that, and rewrite from there. I didn't understand what "rewriting" was, anyway. "Rewriting" always seemed to make my poems *worse.* But by doing this thing over which I didn't have much control, I would see new and sometimes terrific combinations. You have to cheat to make it syntactical, of course, logical and sentence-like.

Basically, it involves treating words as objects, not as conveyors of meaning. Too often you write a poem that says my heart is breaking, the sky is dark, the storm clouds are gathering, let me out of this park: you know, a poem with a strong message which will stink unless it's great art, actually. But sometimes poems get too heavy with message, as if you want to communicate some idea of feeling or thought too much and you forget that it's the same feeling or idea that a hundred million other people have had, and there's nothing so spectacular about it per se. So in art the crux is somewhere else, it's not in the fact of your saying something that everybody else thinks or feels. Like knowing how right you are doesn't make your art any better, that's what I mean.

Now, I'd like to do another writing thing. This is totally different than the things we've done so far, which have been rather mechanical. I want to do something now that's not mechanical at all. This is called "I Remember." Memory is funny. I often wonder why we don't remember everything. It really pisses me off that I can't remember things better. I can't remember the names of poems, I can't remember the names of movies, I have trouble with the names of people, also. I think it would be very nice if I could open my memory, to say, March 12, 1947. I mean I was alive then and I was conscious. But it would be interesting if I could literally just go back to that date in my memory, I mean my mentality must have some kind of impression of that day. But I've found that when I think about the past, like when I was five, say, there are certain things that come out very clearly, and I don't know why they do. Sometimes they're important things—the day I knocked my teeth out on a bicycle, I remember that very well. I also remember the day that some women came to our house. It was raining. My mother was having a Tupperware party in the living room, and there were all these women sitting in our living room: winter and a Tupperware party and the Tupperware saleswoman with her party favors and paraphernalia. Remember Tupperware—do they still have it? Well, it's perfect for the leftovers, in a little bowl, and then you put a plastic lid on it and you push down. And then you "burp" it—remember that, *burping the Tupperware?* You lift this thing and it goes whoosh, ahh, vacuum seal. I remember being fascinated with burping the Tupperware, and I remember the rain outside. And I remember also going out to our back porch and sitting there, I think I was eating, and I heard this clawing noise at the door. And I went and opened the door and there was this really ugly dog totally wet, looking at me, you know, and I was about eight or nine. I let the dog in and I put it in the kitchen and I gave it some food. We didn't have a dog. I don't know what I gave it, probably a peanut butter sandwich. So anyway, I remember feeding the dog, and then I knew that my mother wouldn't want it, you know, it was wet and ugly and horrible, so I said, you know, OK, out you go. Finally, when the Tupperware party was over we opened the door and the dog was still there, and my mother said we could keep it for a couple of days, and then we kept it for about fifteen years. I taught it to walk on its hind legs and to play *Clair de Lune* [*laughter*]. . . . It's not an earthshaking story, yet certain details come into focus so clearly: the color of the dog, the feeling of the wall as I open the back door, the garage wall and the brick, the red brick and the pale green wood. I mean that's very clear, and yet certain other things like the faces of the women I don't remember at all. I just have an impression of bigness and cosmetics. Well anyway, I envy people who can go back that far in memory. I've done some experimenting trying to go back in time, not in any weirdo fashion or "mystical" fashion. I mean you could take it to a mystical point of view if you wanted, it just doesn't matter to me. I remember some things being very important at the time and other things didn't seem to be important at all. I remember at the age of three, pouring a bottle of 7-Up on my Uncle James' head. He'd taken me up on his shoulders in front of my grandparent's cafe, and for some reason I just turned the green bottle upside down and dumped it on his head. And the great thing was, he thought it was hilarious. He loved it.

The thing is, you have to try to screen out the difference between genuine memory, and a secondary memory you have of people telling you what happened. Parents have a way of saying, "When you were little, blah blah blah. . . ." Then twenty years later on, you're under the impression that you remember that. All you have is a visual recreation of what you have been told happened to you. Sometimes it's hard to differentiate between things you remember happening to you and things you were *told* happened to you. This latter type can be quite vivid, and yet totally synthetic or borrowed.

What I'd like you to do now is to go back into your past, as far back as you can. You don't have to get into diapers—something that happened to you a long time ago that you have always remembered clearly. It doesn't have to be important, or poetic or anything like that, just something that you remember that really happened to you. OK? Write down one or two of these memories, and be very specific: instead of "I remember a man on the road," say, "I remember a very fat young man in green suspenders . . ." You could write one long "I Remember" or several short ones. OK, now I am going to read these all aloud. What this will do is give us a kind of collective class memory.

"I remember *I Remember Mama,* a television program, and *One Man's Family,* brought to you by Sweetheart Soap, and *Life of Riley,* coming back from Friday night dinner at Grandma's house and watching *Life of Riley*. Coming back especially in time to see *Life of Riley*. My favorite TV program then. I guess I was past *Howdy Doody* by then. I can't remember whether this was at the same time as *Flash Gordon* or not." I loved *Life of Riley,* myself. I loved his friend, his neighbor; the guy who said "Hi ya, Rile."

Remember that guy? I love that guy. He plays the cab driver in the movie where Humphrey Bogart gets a new face. I love that guy, a very tough guy, actually. He looked like a jerk on that show, but he's a very tough guy and I liked him. OK. That's beautiful, the way he keeps repeating the *Life of Riley,* you really realize that the person really did like the *Life of Riley,* you know, because they dwell on it, "especially in time to see *Life of Riley.*"

"I remember the oversize gloves my brother and I used to box each other with, and my father who laughed while watching us scrap, and the alarm clock he had taken from his bedroom. Our boxing ring was always the livingroom."

I remember boxing with a friend of mine, Dick Gallup, and the first time we hit each other we got pissed off and said "enough of that." It hurts to get hit in the face, you know, what's the point of that?

"I remember the day I first ate a genuine orange. Up until then all I'd ever known about oranges was canned orange juice. But there I was in kindergarten, or first grade, confronted with a real live orange. I didn't have sense enough to look around and see what the other kids were doing with it. I just bit into it, skin and all, and ate the whole thing. The skin tasted bad, but I consumed it. The juice squirted out, but I ate the insides too. Then I had a terrible stomach ache. Followed seconds later by puking up the whole meal. It wasn't until years later that I would touch raw fruit again."

"I remember the day I was called from my college senior class to the hospital and there my father was either dead or very nearly so. Two days earlier, my mother and I had seen him connected to so many tubes and wires. The only other people we'd seen wired up like that always died. My father had known it too. He'd grasped my mother's hand and expressed a need of her presence. That was two days before being called away from school. I got to the hospital. The nurses started weeping when they told me. They liked my father a lot. He was an old southern ladies' man, very good looking too, for his age. I felt numb, no feelings at all, just process. Then my mother came in, called from work. She was crying already. I comforted her, but she was strong too. My father had been sick for two years. The white curtains were drawn around his bed. Suddenly I had the strong urge to look, to see what he would look like dead. We were cremating him, so I'd never get another chance. I looked in. His eyes were covered with gauze. His eyes had been given to science. His mouth was open. The shock produced no reaction. I felt nothing. Just process. But later on, weeks later, I started to react."

That's really incredible, next to the orange, wow.

Next.

"I remember drawing stick figures on the livingroom wall in red crayola."

—It's always red crayola. A friend of mine, Joe Brainard, wrote a book called *I Remember* and it's about one hundred fifty pages long. Every entry begins "I remember . . ." and it's a fantastic book. Anne Waldman and Joan Simon and I published this book. If you don't buy it, you all get flunked out of this course. Anyway, in his *I Remember,* he says I remember the red crayola was always the first one to go. And it's true. Anyway—

"I remember drawing stick figures on the livingroom wall in the red crayola."

"I remember playing chicken in the knives and getting the knife stuck in my big toe, as my mother sat on the balcony watching."

"I remember playing football in the street, and running into the pointed rear fender of a '57 Cadillac, falling on the ground, out of breath and in agony, while a stray dog came up and licked my face."

"I remember leaving my little dog chained to a drugstore door, through three hours of a snowstorm and running back to get him when I realized he was missing."

"I remember hitting my brother over the head with a gun like the cowboys did, and getting my ass kicked for it."

"I remember kicking a female schoolmate in the ass, having her mother come to the house to complain for two hours."

—one for each side, I guess—

"and having my old man kick my ass, because he had missed his favorite TV show."

Wonderful.

"I remember playing football in the alley, kicking the ball into a woman's yard, and having her come out with a butcher knife when I went to get it."

"I remember pounding a little kid's head against a garage, and running eight blocks when his old man came after me. I ran to the carnival."

This person had a particularly rough childhood.

"I remember living out kind of in the country, but not quite. It was a windy afternoon. I was on my tricycle, holding on to a red ballon on a string. Accidentally, I let go of it and it sailed off down the street I lived on across Long Pine, a small black-top highway, across railroad tracks and a field. I wanted to go running after it, but all the people around said, 'Nope, it's gone forever.' "

I remember that feeling, yeah, the first time you realize something is *gone forever.* I remember very well leaving the sixth grade. It was a big deal, you know. But I remember thinking, I'll never be in the sixth grade again. And I remember just being impressed. That was very impressive, it wasn't good or bad, it was just there, like Mount Rushmore.

"I remember walking along a ledge of a cement wall. It was dark, and there was black water on both sides. My grandmother was with me."

—strange family—

"suddenly a little green snake crawled over the path and slid down into the water. My grandmother said to be careful of snakes. She once kicked one in the hay while she followed her father, cutting with a scythe in a field. It was poisonous and she had a swollen leg for weeks. The same day, I fell on a rock and cut my knee bloodily. My oldest scar, but it's almost disappeared."

"I remember being on my uncle's cabin cruiser and sleeping while everyone else was fishing."

"I remember accidentally stabbing a boy in the first grade with a pencil. I remember the Sister getting very angry and making me kneel in front of the class."

"I remember watching a cartoon on the TV where you bought a piece of plastic to put over the TV, drawing in lines, bridges, etc., to help the character escape danger."

—boy, that—do you remember that, does anyone remember that? You could buy plastic shields, you stick them on the thing. And there was a show, and you participated. You get a clear plastic sheet which stuck to the TV picture tube and you could draw on it with erasable crayons. The TV would say, "Look, storm coming, maybe lightning will hit the wolf!" Then you draw a jagged line down to the wolf, and then there'd be an explosion and the wolf would disappear. It was beautiful, you know. I had forgotten all about that.

"I remember the first time I got to spend the night at another person's house. This person was a girl about my age, six or seven, and she had brown hair and lived across the field from our house. I was at her house that evening, eating cherries and looking at the Catholic religious objects, and wondering what they meant. I remember being a little anxious about how to behave, and, after we went to bed, I woke up knowing I'd wet the bed, which at that age, it'd been impressed on me, was very bad. I must have carried some regrets about that night, because about a year later upon returning from a vacation with my parents, she came over to greet me and I pissed all over her before she could get away."

The last word on this paper is "UGH!" Hey, you're not sitting in the front row, are you?

"I remember hiding on the floor of our '55 Chevy: dark, dark green. I always thought it was black. Hiding from all the spectators that came to see my brother's room burn up, and claiming objects thrown out the window by the firemen. I remember guarding the pile of objects later."

—do you remember when you could get down on the floor boards and hide? And you could sit there. That was nice.

"I remember when a girl friend hit her head on our cement steps. We were playing 'Red Rover Red Rover will someone come over.' She was bleeding and I had to get a neighbor friend, a nurse, because the girl kept fainting. My mother was flipping out and the nurse had the girl smell a bottle of ammonia. I remember being afraid for my friend because the smell was so horrible; I knew she would survive from the cut, but maybe die from the ammonia."

"I remember in the first grade, I threw up on my workbook. I don't really remember throwing up, but I remember realizing that I had. The teacher got some other kid's raincoat and put it on me backwards holding it around me at the back of my neck and dragged me down the hall. As we went down the hall, she reprimanded me for drinking chocolate milk at break-time."

"I remember the first time I ever colored inside the lines. It was in our old house which was huge. I got lost in the endless guest rooms, terrifying, quite often. Exploring the house was a big event. Anyway, I had a huge English woman for a nanny. She was eighty years old and six feet tall. I used to hug her around the knees a lot. We were sitting at the huge old red table in the playroom. It was raining outside. And the afternoon was well along. Nanny was wonderful. She would actually play *with* me. She was coloring too. Coloring book. Picture of a pig, I think. Coloring. I am coloring all over the place because the crayon's too big for my hand. Then I look over at Nanny's picture. I like hers better. A poodle, I think. I notice that the poodle is blue against the white page, and I start to color another picture, a cat, and I stay inside the lines. It was like a flash of enlightenment."

"I remember my favorite game when I was in kindergarten. The plot was very simple. It required only one other person to play with. The two of us would pretend that we were very little babies who had been abandoned in a deep dark wood by cruel parents. We would crawl through this fantasy wood, crying, pretending that we were lost and hungry. Then, all of a sudden, we would find ourselves in a clearing in which there was a huge house whose doors were wide open. We would crawl in and find in the house everything we had ever dreamed of: toys, candy, chocolate milk, soft beds, and warm sunshine. At that point, when, as babies, we were gurgling with glee, the plan of the game ended. Actually, we never got beyond that, because although we planned the game for some time, we only got to play once. The game required only two people to play it: me and my friend Donna Magworth, who was skinny like me, and also had a big brown ponytail like me. But it required absolutely *all* the toys in the kindergarten. We used the big, foot-long cardboard blocks that looked like bricks to make the walls of the house. We used the little blocks to make the shelves of the house and we used the dolls and the toy airplanes and tea sets and toy cart and everything. Then, the one time we played it, we spent what seemed like hours wrestling all the toys away from every other kid in the room and blocking off our game area: the whole room. When we finally got around to starting, crawling along the grey wood floor, forest floor rug, a howl went up from every corner of the room, where all the other kids had been assigned by us. That caught the teacher's attention and it broke up the whole game. Just as we entered the magic house, we were scolded and the other kids were comforted. And as punishment, we had to sit in the corner and 'read the books,' which amounted to just sitting in the corner since we couldn't even read yet."

These are great, aren't they? Do you like these? I love them.

"I remember when I lived on a farm in Wisconsin and had just gotten a B-B gun. I used to walk over to my friend's house and shoot pigeons in her barn. She was really cute and had a really smart older sister who looked stupid. One day I remember having shot her in the hip, somehow, up in the hayloft. And how exciting it was when she pulled her pants down to show me the B-B mark. So, one day, she was in the old outhouse her father had made into a playhouse"

—what an anal family! Anyway, she was out in the converted outhouse. . . .

"and I was in the yard, and I saw her peeking out at me through a crack in the boards, and without hesitation I thought how funny it would be to shoot her between the eyes, but knew I was too far away. I took careful aim and fired. I heard a scream, and saw a little red spot between her eyes, as she ran out of the outhouse. I never saw her again."

"When I was seven perhaps, I remember going to a great uncle's farm near Winnipeg, Manitoba."

—I love the way the Canadians put the name of the province. Notice that with the other one? Vancouver, British Columbia. Anyway, it's not Vancouver, Arkansas. This one is a great uncle's farm near Winnipeg, Manitoba.

"It was summer and my mother called her brother, maternal grandparents, my cousin Leah, and perhaps her sister, Sharon: they were all there. While everyone stayed on the porch, my cousin and another little girl, who wore a white dress, were swinging on a big hammock around the side of the house. It was muddy there, and I decided to walk in the fields. My father came along and we picked peas and shelled them and ate them. The peas were sweet, sweeter than any peas I've eaten since. I got a terrific stomachache and my father had to carry me back to the house. I think I fell in love with the girl in the white dress, but I'm not sure. She was the grand-daughter of my great uncle whose name I just can't remember."

—very pretty scene. I would like to have been there.

"I remember, eight years old, I remember living at 123rd Street and Dove, Dove Avenue, next to the corner, and some people who lived in the back of the store in a small brick house, with a fenced-in backyard to keep their two-year-old son, Chuckie, and an old brown bulldog, fat-lipped Duchess, in the yard. One day my sister Gloria and I were playing with a tennis ball in the driveway and heard Chuckie scream. Usually, he'd ride on Duchess' back, but now,

Duchess, on her hind legs, was riding Chuckie all over the yard. He kept trying to shake her, but she kept breaking her fall and would latch on with her front legs. She wasn't trying to hurt him, but just in it for the ride. We laughed hysterically until his mother finally put an end to Duchess. Chuckie would always throw his red tennis shoes over the fence onto our roof, then cry and ask us to get them, while he munched his Cocoa Crispies."

"I remember, nine years old, playing catch with a football with a black fullback who was working on the city street in front of our house. He could really run and pass the ball to me easy enough for me to hold on to it.

"I remember my earliest recollection, being when I was about three. We were in Southampton on vacation. Most of it is sketchy, something to do with a Dugan truck, another to do with an abandoned, half-sunken boat, and someone eating crabs and snapping their claws at me. The most vivid memory was that I was playing outside in the dirt with some toy trucks, when the lady who ran the cottage we were staying at informed me that I was playing in poison ivy. I remember the lady as being one of those vast, dykish women who in my child mind I always thought were truck drivers"

—many are.

"I remember the most vivid dream I ever had occurred when I was in grade school. I haven't the slightest idea of the date, year, or grade, however. The dream began, realistically enough, with my waking up in the morning, going through all of the preschool preparations and walking to school. Being a Catholic school, it was the custom to begin the day with prayers. Everything was perfectly real, save that instead of praying to a crucifix, for some reason we were aiming our prayers at St. Francis. The statues of this saint almost always depict him with his arms sort of folded in front of him with clenched fists. While praying I noticed the statue spreading his fingers, first on one hand, and then on the other. Petrified, I looked about me. All were praying as usual. No one noticed. I rubbed my eyes. Next, the figure began to stretch his arms and yawn, smiling evilly at me.

People were still praying. No one saw it but me. I ran around the room shaking people, screaming, 'The statue moved, the statue moved.' I woke up shaking my pillow, screaming at it."

"I remember the autumn of 1959. We lived in New York, and my father had, in some mysterious way, gotten tickets for the Yankees-Pirates World Series. The subtle electricity of autumn, the electricity of the World Series, eyes glued to TVs and ears cocked to the radios. Reports of the scores slipped surreptitiously through our desk ranks as we squirmed in the seats. Saturday, game day. Crowds jammed so tight in the subway. My father looked concerned and held us close, fearing we'd be trampled in the headlong breathless rush up the ramps into Yankee Stadium. Golden, golden is the color I remember. It seemed to hang in a haze over the stadium. The golden autumn, the golden boys, the Yankees. Bobby Richardson hitting a grand slam home run, barely dropping into the left field seats, the trouncing of the Pirates, my joy. The next day, tenacious Pirates, tenaciously held on and edged by the Yankees. The week zoomed by. The Yankees would mash the Pirates, and then the Pirates would squeak out another victory. The final game. I had to endure the confines of the school. The game see-sawed. My desk see-sawed. The final bell sounded. I ran to my bicycle foresaking my companions, racing home so fast, I was standing up pedaling, when I neared the corner, I heard a shout. Mazerowsky hit a homer! The Pirates won, the Pirates won! I sagged on the bike and rode slowly home."

"I remember sleeping in a hammock on the Trans-Europe express, speeding through the nights and days. My parents were taking me on a pilgrimage, and a Catholic Bishop, staying in the same compartment, told them on his faith that he had never before through his young life seen such a young pilgrim. My parents got very proud, they told me, years and years later they came out again with this same story as often as possible. The Bishop gave me a blessing on the forehead and it felt cold. That's all I remember and that's the meaning the word blessing kept having for me until fairly recently—cold."

"I remember walking behind Brenda, she was three and I was five, and noticing the hair on her back. She is half Okinawan. Okinawans are a fairly hairy race, and Brenda's black back hair was very visible in the sunlight. We walked down the slope past the green porch towards the cattails. The yard of the Puerto Rican woman next door was overgrown. The plants crowded together on the ground seemed almost to set off little explosions. The green banana and pork pateris"—what is that word, does anybody know? What does it mean? Fried, right?—"The green banana and pork pateris she made were certainly explosive. The red peppers sent you running to the bathroom. Brenda is a hairdresser today, living in California."

That's beautiful. It's so visual you can picture it happening. I also like the way you get to know what happened to the person today. It's very interesting—somebody you knew when you were six. Like you meet them now: they're selling Buicks? You know, then you think of yourself, and they must think you're even odder, whatever you're doing. You're a poet? What exactly is that? Anyway, I got a few more to read. Are you getting tired? I'll try to read them quickly and no blah blah blah in between.

"I remember coming in the house from the snow and standing by the wood stove to take off my wet boots."

"I remember laying on a table, the smell of ether, a buzzing in my ears: my mother holding my hand, and me waking up with a burning throat."

"I remember watching my brother standing up to pee in the toilet. I remember catching bees in hollyhocks and throwing them at my brother. I remember holding a little bird that shit in my hand."

"I remember I could throw stones from my house front door and hit the cars on Crayton Road. Crayton Road was big enough to have the buses run on it, but I never threw stones at the double deckers because the drivers, who were tough, from Glasgow, would stop the whole bus and get out and chase whoever it was. Once one of the regular buses went up and down Crayton Road for days with the back window shattered by a golf ball: from Crayton Golf Course, which was right against Crayton Road. Golf balls were always flying out, and we boys would go out and down a hedge beside the road looking for them. Then we'd give them back to the golfers, expecting a couple of pennies. Or go around to neighborhood doors, selling them very cheap. Between Crayton Road and my house, which was on Crayton Gardens, there was a green strip owned by the borough of Milgraves, where we used to play French cricket. We let Juan Berg play because he had the bat. Sometimes lovely Christine Murray would play. Especially on summer nights. And we were calling her 'Murray-mints, Murray-mints, too good for hurry mints.' And she was kept in the house all the time and her family was so poor, we used to give them leftovers for their cat, Flossie. Late at night, Mrs. Murray, a very thin, shriveled woman, would go out, especially as we heard a cat screaming, and yell, 'Flossie, Flossie, come in here right now.' Mr. Murray was a deaf mute we never saw."

"I remember being with my brother in the bathtub. We used to take baths together all the time. But this day, we had been fighting all day. We used to fight all the time, and loved it. Anyway, since he was bigger than I was, I had to be very clever in our fights or trick him. This time in the bathtub, I bit what I thought was his hand. It came off in my mouth."

I— don't know if I want to go on with this one.

"I was at once very pleased with myself, and of course horrified that I'd get into trouble for biting off my brother's fingers. It was, I discovered as I chewed, a bar of soap he had rapidly substituted for his hand."

"I remember when the king of Morocco came to my town. I got all dressed up in my best shorts and knee socks. Shoes polished, I went over to where he was arriving for lunch. All the press people, including photographers were there. When the limousines arrived, this very bizarre looking man in a fez got out, surrounded by military guards, etc. I pushed my way through the crowd and went up to him and introduced myself. We walked hand-in-hand up the long steps of the restaurant, and stood at the top of the stairs waving very slowly back and forth, royal style, as the photographers went wild. They loved me. I was five years old."

"I remember the time when I was six or seven years old, and my aunt and uncle, whom I lived with, had a big fight. It was surely one of the largest they'd ever had. Dishes, glasses, beer bottles, broken candles, and the shaking of my aunt in mid-air. And my uncle trembling with drunken emotional rage, running out the door, lest he lose all his control. I remember this all so vividly, because for many days, weeks, and months, and even years, we looked back at this past mood many times: sometimes with fear, but later with humor. I always used to kid them with 'Remember the Big Fight?' "

—they must have loved you.

"I also remember around the same age period, mood, stage of my life, a more simple occurrence with my father, who was a one-time cop driving in his car. I repeatedly insisted, 'if you're really a cop, go drive through the red light, c'mon.' He just smiled and laughed to himself and did."

"I remember climbing the steps of my father's New Jersey home, turning the corner with my Halloween mask and ghoulish costume, and terrifying my iguana lizard into performing agile acrobatics in his cage."

"I remember chucking an apple down a road, waiting twelve seconds, and listening to the smack sound as it hit the right leg of my best friend. About twelve seconds later, I was rubbing my leg."

"I remember hyperventilating in a den of a red brick colonial house."

—those two things, the house and the hyperventilation, they really go together in some mysterious way.

"I remember kissing Wendy, a beautiful third grader, behind the fourth tree from the corner of Central and Greenville streets, Madison, New Jersey."

"I remember the time my grandfather was accused of shoplifting at Food Town, a big supermarket. His face was stricken. Later, he said his heart had really gone crazy."

"I remember wanting to kiss a girl named Barbara Logsden. She was so pretty, with brown hair and eyes. I remember kissing her, finally: a little peck on the forehead. I remember hating myself later for being such a chicken. I remember seeing her ten or twelve years later on the street. We walked right past each other. She never raised her eyes. She was so beautiful. I remember thinking just that, as I stared at the grass growing in the cracks in the sidewalk. I remember preferring sidewalks that said WPA on them to those that didn't, because my grandfather had worked on the WPA pouring concrete"

—God, those are, aren't those beautiful? Those are really nice, you know. We've written this work of genius today. That was beautiful, very beautiful. Anybody want to say anything about this?

Q: I kept getting all sorts of flashes back as you were reading.

R.P.: Yeah, it'll do it. And you know, some of the stuff I read there applied to me. These are individual memories, but if they're genuine memories of genuine things that actually happened to you, if you don't try to fake it, you'll find that they're really memories that most everyone has. They're almost like the collective unconscious on the level of memory or something. It's odd, but it's true.

Well listen, I want to recommend two books to you. There are a lot of nice writing suggestions in them. I say suggestions because I can't relate to people who say you should write *one way*. Advice is good, it's wonderful, and it's especially good if it's from your friends, people who know you and can tell when you're faking. A lot of times people who are well-meaning, such as myself, will give you the feeling that you should do things their way, without saying so directly. They project on to you, you know. I mean, look here, me teacher, you student, that kind of thing. This guy must know something, he's standing up there talking, and we're sitting out here listening, right? You notice that feeling? Take in what you can, but don't let anybody railroad you. Finally, here are the names of two books with about one hundred different, weird, and interesting writing ideas. If you're interested you can find them, or just have to write away for them. They have corny names, but, what can you do. They're *The Whole Word Catalogue* and *The Whole Word Catalogue 2,* available from Teachers & Writers Collaborative, 186 West 4th Street, New York City, 10014, four dollars and seven dollars, respectively. OK, I guess I should stop now.

Sources

BRAINARD, JOE, *I Remember* (New York: Full Court Press, 1975). Reprinted by permission of the publisher.

Photo by Andrea Craig

Clark Coolidge

ARRANGEMENT

JULY 19, 1977

I HOPE WE can all be reasonably comfortable here. I know we're all packed in and there are no windows. But also I feel a little "back here and up above you," which I don't intend to be symbolic or whatever.

First I should say I'm very honored and pleased to be asked to be here among poets like Allen Ginsberg and Gregory Corso and William Burroughs who have been my teachers, even though I haven't sat in their classes except in the case of Allen in Vancouver in 1963. But also I have certain doubts I must admit up front about being somebody who dispenses any kind of absolutely-applicable-to-everybody information.

"Visiting Poets" is a very accurate term. I'm a poet. I'm not a professional teacher. I've never taught in this way before. I do believe that by telling you what I've experienced and all the things that have turned me on, I might possibly be of use to you. This is going to be quite rapid in places. I'm going to try and give you as much information as I have, in the sense of trying to give you some options. I think it's very important to know how many possibilities there are for an artist, and there are almost too many. There *are* too many. So, if the information goes by you quickly or there are things, names, that you're not familiar with, I hope you'll ask me and I'll be glad to try to amplify.

The form of this will be, I'll come and present something each time. I'll be playing you some music, reading some work by myself and others, talking about it, and then you'll be free to ask questions or discuss whatever I've been talking about.

I'm also very pleased to be the first part of a course with Philip Whalen who also has been a teacher of mine, in a sense, a very great poet and beautiful man, to whom I feel I particularly owe a lot of the delight I have in the process of writing, and I feel that Philip communicates that in particular.

I wanted to start with a subject I think is basic to my work and to art, I presume. That's the word "arrangement." I'm partly using that word because I want to avoid using words like "composition," "structure," and so on, which I don't feel mean much any more. I think the problem with talking about art is that art is so particular that you want to talk concretely and precisely. It's very hard to do that all the time. You've got to generalize sometimes, but the process of working is a particular process. You're dealing with words, one word at a time, with all the circuits that are in your mind, with all the things that impinge on you. How do you put them together. All right, the word "arrangement"—hear the word "range" in that word—a field which I think we've been given as artists since the fifties in this country by men as diverse as Charles Olson and John Cage, from two sides. You might even think of them as the positive and negative, or make a figure like that. I'll be talking more about them.

But when I was thinking about giving this course I tried to think back to things that were important starts in my work as an artist. I've tried to go back as far as possible, and I've found a story that I read when I was in junior high school. I was a science fiction nut then, partly because of a kind of nervous boredom that prevailed then, and I don't think I was learning anything about scholastic material. I read thousands of science fiction books, one after the other, huge shelves of them, anything: Heinlein, Ray Bradbury, Theodore Sturgeon, all those people. So anyway, there was this story, and I'll just read you a few paragraphs of it because I think this is one of the things that really started me off, even though it was years before I ever wrote anything.

This story's called *Mimsy Were the Borogroves* by Lewis Padgett, who also went by the name of Henry Kuttner. In the story, in the beginning, a little boy named Scott, who's ten years old, is playing down by a creek and finds these strange objects, and these objects are toys, they're instructional toys that came from another planet in the future. He doesn't know that, but he takes them home and he and his sister Emma, who's about five years old, start playing with them, and these toys start working on their minds and changing them from human beings into . . . what? So I'll just read you part of the last three pages of this.

> Scott kept bringing gadgets to Emma for her approval. Usually she'd shake her head. Sometimes she would signify agreement. Then there would be an hour of laborious, crazy scribbling on scraps of note paper, and Scott, after studying the notations, would arrange and rearrange his rocks, bits of machinery, candle ends, and assorted junk. Each day the maid cleaned them away, and each day Scott began again.
>
> He condescended to explain a little to his puzzled father, who could see no rhyme or reason in the game.
>
> "But why this pebble right here?"
>
> "It's hard and round, Dad. It *belongs* there."
>
> "So is this one hard and round."
>
> "Well, that's got vaseline on it. When you get that far, you can't *see* just a hard, round thing."
>
> "What comes next? This candle?"
>
> Scott looked disgusted. "That's toward the end. The iron ring's next."
>
> It was, Paradine [*that's the father*] thought, like a scout trail through the woods, markers in a labyrinth. But here again was the random factor. Logic halted—

familiar logic—at Scott's motives in arranging the junk as he did.

. . . .

An hour later a clatter of feet upstairs roused him from his doze. Scott's voice was crying exultantly, "This is it, Slug! Come on!" [*Slug was a name for his sister.*]

. . . Paradine grimaced. What the devil was going on upstairs?

Scott shrieked, "Look out! This way!"

Paradine . . . raced up the stairs. The door of Scott's room was open.

The children were vanishing.

They went in fragments, like thick smoke in a wind, or like movement in a distorting mirror. Hand in hand they went, in a direction Paradine could not understand, and as he blinked there on the threshold, they were gone.

. . . on the carpet lay a pattern of markers, pebbles, an iron ring—junk. A random pattern.

Now to me, that's a very stiff shot at something that still involves me in ways I never could have understood *then,* because I wasn't writing. But actually I'd started as a musician. I started playing the drums when I was in the third grade grammar school band and went on through to play in symphony-type situations and bebop drums and rock-and-roll in David Meltzer's Serpent Power band in San Francisco, in 1967. So anyway, I must have had some sense of arrangement in terms of music, but not yet in writing. And that story now comes back to me with all the feelings of great discovery and mystery and desire to do something with this [*picks up piece of chalk, a book, etc.*] . . . and this . . . and this. Where do I put it? What happens when I put it there? What does it do to *this?* How close is it? Does it repel me? Does it repel you? How much does it weigh down the table? Can I look through it? What do I see when I look through it, and another whole vector of stuff coming in visually? Anyway, it took years to begin to articulate that in a form of art.

I should also say that when I was very young, about six years old, my parents took me to a natural history museum in Boston, which is no longer there. But it was a marvelous place, great big old red brownstone building with dark rooms. I see them as if they were covered with black velvet inside, and with beautiful glass cases with buttons that you push and lights come on and wonderful objects inside. Imagine, six years old, and there it is—minerals! Crystals, quartz, calcite, agates, opals—things; I didn't know what they were. Push the button, see this arrangement. And the minerals themselves as an arrangement of molecules, the axes of a crystal. They are distinct substances, and they have powers. I'm reminded of—probably some of you have read Castaneda—the business about finding your spot. Where is it? Where is the spot where your power can most come out of you, be of most use? I think the problem is, though, that there is not *a* spot. There are *spots*. More than one. I don't want to use the word *form* here, I want to use the word *forms*. The word is plural, always plural. You never have just one. In fact, sometimes there is a desire to have one, but unh-unh, something always comes. But thank God it does.

So I began to look at minerals and I began to collect them, and I remember my folks bought me one of those little boxes with the cardboard dividers and little specimens. Little dollar tiny box, calcite crystal, put it on a page and see how the words doubled. Okay, I took that home and I began to go out and find rocks, began to bug my parents to take me out on Saturday to quarries and my father didn't want to go; he wanted to stay home and listen to the Metropolitan Opera broadcast, and I had to go out to some quarry and pick up rocks. I began to learn the names. And not just the names but where they came from, what they were made of. You understand, I had no desire to do anything with this to be professional. Later I did, but at this point it was just pure fascination. What *are* those things?

In fact, I remember a funny incident in Providence, Rhode Island, where Brown University is. Because my father was professor of music there, I got to know the chairman of the geology department. He used to let me go and open the drawers and look at all the minerals. And I remember being in there one day and there were these guys and they were all working with Bunsen burners and blowpipes and everything and they were smashing rocks with hammers and they were taking a test, an exam. I was in junior high school and they were in sophomore year or something, and one of them saw me looking through the drawers and he said, "Hey, come here, what is this?" "Sure," I said, "that's an apatite crystal from Ontario." He said, "Thank you," and he wrote it down. So I got chastised of course: "Don't do that, this is a serious test." But I remember it struck me that they were going through all these procedures, these rules they were taught; that you burn the thing and you get the bead of it, you put it in a solution, it turns a certain color, you write something down, there's mathematics, and *then* you find out. I didn't have to do that. I picked the thing up, I looked at it, I held it in my hand, maybe I sniffed it, maybe I licked it, and I knew what it was and I knew where it was from, just purely from looking and touching and having them. This was the way I learned this. Now, alright, this gave me trouble with education.

That's another reason I feel strange here, because I hated school and in fact I had two years of a major in geology. I got to the point where I thought maybe I would become a geologist but when I found out what geologists do, it wasn't what I had imagined. I had a very romantic image, I guess. I thought I would be standing in the Gobi Desert with a pick, finding dinosaur eggs or something, like Roy Chapman Andrews. And, no, that's not what it is, you know. I mean, when I did this, I hit the school and majored in geology just at the time when, in the late fifties, geology was changing from being a descriptive science to a real high-toned mathematical, geophysical, super-laboratory stress-and-strain type science. Anybody who looked at rocks and collected minerals and got something out of that . . . Forget it. I'd get in the laboratory, look through the microscope, "Yeah, sure." Slide rule.

And these guys were so dull. I remember this one guy, he was an expert on foraminifera, tiny little—they call them forams, maybe some of you know them. Tiny shelled creatures that lived in early Paleozoic time. He went down to the basement all the time and he took these rocks and he smashed them up with a hammer and took these tiny things out and put them in trays, classifying them. That's all he did. He didn't read the newspapers or anything. He wore gum shoes that made a funny sticking sound when he walked by. It was really terrible. So I was disabused of any notion of being one of these people. I mean, I'm not trying to indict . . . I've met geologists since that were pretty hip people, but gee, the line of them didn't look that way then. I saw some of their wives too. A Geology Wife . . . that's . . . that was actually a term we used to use. Anyway, I'm far afield but maybe not.

So, the minerals. Very early I saw reproductions of the works of Yves Tanguy, who you may know is one of the surrealist painters who came to this country during the war and lived in Connecticut, and who painted landscapes where the horizon is maybe not there. You can't quite tell. It seems to be a slanting plane. It may be on the water, it may be the desert, but anyway, there are these forms. Are they mineral, are they animal, are they about to move or are they frozen there since before time? Fantastic. They're placed. There's an arrangement. I saw these and I felt what I would call now a recognition. Isn't it Duncan who talks about recognition? When you see something you've never seen before and you know that it's going to be of use to you and part of you; you recognize it. There's something in you that is ready for that, that is circuited or whatever, that is connected correctly so that you glom onto that thing right away. I did that with Tanguy, before I really knew anything about painting or aesthetics.

In fact, Tanguy—this is a little bit of a digression, but one of his juvenile paintings, which is reproduced in the Museum of Modern Art catalogue for his first show there, shows an ocean liner. It's a kid's painting. It's primitive. It's too long, it has endless rows of little windows. Like, I was in first grade during the Second World War and we used a lot of red crayon. We had the Jap Zeros being shot down and the submarines, and the pictures were all filled up with red. You liked to draw big fighting ships and put in millions of windows. You get totally involved in that, you forgot what it was all about, what was the story? So, anyway, Tanguy had this painting of this ship which seemed to be stretched incredibly out. Now, I did recognize this because I had recurrent dreams that were exactly that image. In fact, it would go from a concrete image of that to a strange, sucking kind of force-field thing, which can't exist in this state. It's been described to me as possibly intra-uterine dreams. In other words, dreams of being in the womb. I don't know whether I accept that, but think about it. So Tanguy was a great influence.

And then, to continue the painting, in the fifties I saw reproductions of Philip Guston's paintings that he painted in the early fifties. Do any of you know Philip Guston's work at all? His paintings in the fifties were grey fields with many red or pinkish marks tending to be clustered. In fact, they remind me a bit of Mondrian's "Plus and Minus" or "Sea" pictures; in fact, these influenced Guston. These marks would tend to cluster and center, off-balance, and he would repaint. He would take them out, paint them over with grey or white, and the grey would get mixed up with the pink and so on. Well, later I met Philip Guston and he's become a good friend. And incidentally, he's one of the best readers I have of my own work. He is a great reader and I think a painter who is a reader is a terrific reader of writing. He does not have the preconceptions that writing must be "this, that, or the other." He looks at it as fresh. Here's a quote from Philip Guston talking about those paintings:

> It cannot be a settled, fixed image. It must of necessity be an image which is unsettled, which has not only not made up its mind where to be but must feel as if it's been in many places all over this canvas, and indeed there's no place for it to settle—except momentarily.

The thing has either just moved or is about to move, that's the sensation you get. I'll probably talk about him again. He's on my mind a lot.

Now music. Notes, frequencies, vibrations, positions on a scale. Arrangements of notes. Charlie Parker playing different intervals from a chord, what have become known as more outer intervals than those that were played before. Thinking of musical space as an arrangement of frequencies, of course, in time. And Schoenberg, on the other side, written music, realizing that there were twelve tones that could be used as an organizing principle instead of tonally-centered seven-note scales. And then there's John Cage and Charles Olson. I think I was aware of John Cage earlier. I know that a Merce Cunningham performance in Providence in the early sixties was a tremendous experience for me, and John was there, and David Tudor, and Robert Rauschenberg was traveling with them and making up the decor of the dances from pieces of stuff that were right there, wherever they went. They went on a tour of colleges. I'll never forget John Cage's music for one of the dances. There was a hall with an aisle down the center and two aisles down the sides with that rubber, those rubber strips that are serrated. You know, you've seen them. He took a window-stick that he found there and placed the metal tip in touch with the serrated rubber and walked very slowly backwards, not crashing into things, down the main aisle making a sound, very softly, you could hardly hear it, and around the back of the room and then down the other aisle and across the front. This took maybe twenty minutes, and that was the music. Invention. And awareness of what was there in the environment that he could use, and a pattern that was already laid out that he could follow. Anyway, that impressed me a great deal.

Merce Cunningham's dances themselves, in fact he had a dance called *Field Dances,* which pretty much described what he did. I don't know if you know his work, but one of the things he did was detach body movement from story framework so that what you see is the gestures and movements, the possibilities of the body, arranged. In arrangement. I can see that word is not going to last very long.

Jumping back a little bit, I became a cave explorer, and that sort of came out of my interest in minerals. My folks took me to Luray Caverns in Virginia when I was about ten years old. Well, it's a beautiful cave full of orange and red stalactites, totally covered with these beautiful and weird formations. And incidentally, in a later class I'll be playing a tape of a very strange musical instrument that they have there, which they call "The Stalacpipe Organ." What they've done is they've tapped, sounded, all the stalactites on the ceiling of this one big room and placed little electric hammers next to them that are attached to a keyboard. In fact, they've even cheated a little bit. They've filed off a little bit of the calcite to tune the note a little better, which I'm not so sure about. So they have this organ console and they play things like "Shenandoah," and I'll be playing you a rendition of "Beautiful Dreamer," which is actually very beautiful.

Anyway, the caves. I got very involved, to the point of joining the National Speleological Society, which is a group that keeps news between cavers moving, and exchange of maps and equipment and so on. And when I was in high school I got very involved with caves in Tennessee and Virginia; I used to go down there in the summertime. And some of these caves had thirty or forty miles of passageways. You would go in and crawl and climb and use ropes and go down shafts that were wet and were muddy and follow where it went. In a cave you can't tell where you're going and it's totally dark, except you have a flashlight if you've provided for yourself properly, and a carbide lamp which burns acetylene and is actually better than a flashlight, brighter. The rock has been cut by water, which has followed the line of least resistance, of softest rock. Layers of water have sunk down. There are levels. You're following the result of a natural process. You go where *it* goes. I think that connects with arrangement in a way.

From that, I think about the arrangement of the actual world. This *stuff*. You know, not microscopic, not atomic. That's another arrangement, which scientists seem to make symmetrical and even. I'm not so sure if it is, but they say so. Although I love some of the names that they use for things: "charms" is one of the new particles which is within the electron now. The smaller they get, the more particles there are. But the actual world is what I think we deal with as artists, or as anybody. Now what I mean by the "actual world" is that you look out your window and you see trees, and leaves on the trees, and birds. Now, where are *they*? What kind of pattern do they make? What sort of arrangement? There seems to be no intelligence behind it but there *is* an arrangement. There are places in space being occupied and moving. In fact, I was recently looking out the window at some birds and I imagined that space was a fabric and that each bird was attached to a place on that fabric, and they were all in motion, all the birds, but they never let the fabric in between them go slack, if you can imagine. Anyway, that's the actual world.

So, geology. I'm reminded of a story. I was once in Cambridge with Aram Saroyan who some of you may know of, who at that time was writing one-word poems. He would sit and smoke some dope and type one word and sit and look at it for hours and take it out and type it again. Originally they were words like "oxygen" and then one day the word "leukemia" appeared . . . Anyway, I left for California at that point and got involved with rock-and-roll. But I was sitting there with Aram, and Robert Creeley, the poet, was visiting. Aram is a person who has to exactly know and exactly state, "I know you," this sort of thing. He looked at me and said, "I know what your work is. I know exactly what you're doing." I said "Huh?," and he said, "It's a big cliff of rock. That's what it is." And I thought and I said, "Yeah," and Creeley sort of looked at us. And later I thought about it and I thought that it was a tremendous misconception because what he thought of it as, is that you look at the rock as just one thing. It's a cliff, okay? You go do something else. The way I look at it, because I've had geological interests and some training, is that geologists *read* the rocks. They can read the layers by the fossils in them and what ages and what came first and sometimes there are very complicated arrangements of strata and faults and things, and they can read what came first even though it's all messed up. So when Aram said "Your works are like cliffs of rock," I thought, yeah, that's right. They have that particular solid separate arrangement aspect and I *read* them, and I want people to read them. And he was saying that you don't have to read them, just look at them. So we agreed, but we were totally wrong, which is an artistic problem too. I have a quotation from Heraclitus here:

> The most beautiful world is like a heap of rubble tossed down in confusion.

Has anyone seen Jean-Luc Godard's films? Have you seen *La Chinoise*? There's an exchange in there that hits me particularly. It's between a boy and a girl: "Guillaume," played by Jean-Pierre Leaud; and "Veronique," played by Anne Wiazemski.

> Guillaume says: People ought to be blind.
> and Veronique: Why?
> Well, it would be better when we speak with each other. We would listen to each other seriously.
> Oh, how is that?
> Language would be redistributed differently. Listen, don't forget that over the last two thousand years words have considerably changed their meanings.

> So?
>
> So, we would converse seriously, because if we were blind, it would be meanings that would change words.
>
> Ah, yes, I understand. To talk to each other as if words were sounds and matter.
>
> That is what they are, Veronique.

Now don't hear that "sounds and matter" as any simplification or abstraction: sounds and matter: emotions, feelings, desires, densities, substance, arrangement. Everything is there.

Ah, I forgot something. Along the way from the *Mimsy Were the Borogroves* story (this connects with it), I began to read H.P. Lovecraft. Does anybody know of him? Yeah, okay, he's become popular recently. But I only knew about him then because I lived in Providence, and he was born and lived in Providence all his life. I knew the houses where he lived and the streets he walked, some of which were the same streets which Poe walked, and he knew it. Anyway, he wrote things like this. He's one of the interesting bad writers. He was influenced by writers like Lord Dunsany, Algernon Blackwood, and Poe. He often has a flowery, sort of stupid, style. But he has some notions about things in his imagination. Listen to part of his story *The Call of Cthalhu.*

> There had been eons when other Things ruled on the earth, and They had had great cities. Remains of Them were still to be found as Cyclopean stones on islands in the Pacific. They all died vast epochs of time before man came, but there were arts which could revive Them when the stars had come round again to the right positions in the cycle of eternity. These Great Old Ones were not composed altogether of flesh and blood. They had shape, but that shape was not made of matter. When the stars were right, They could plunge from world to world through the sky; but when the stars were wrong, They could not live.

Now the phrase, "the stars were right" stuck in. I think you can see the connection with arrangement and Lewis Padgett's story. "When the stars were right," Arrangement, but *what* arrangement? Some more Lovecraft, this time from *The Lurker at the Threshold.*

> Of all this, only the slightest memory, because of what I saw framed in that opening where I had expected to see but stars, and the charnel, nauseating smell that poured in from *Outside*—not stars, but *suns,* great globes of light massing toward the opening, and not alone these, but the breaking apart of the nearest globes, and the protoplasmic flesh that flowed blackly outward to join together and form that eldritch [*that's a word he loves*], hideous horror from outer space, that spawn of the blankness of primal time, that tentacled amorphous monster which was the lurker at the threshold, whose mask was as a congeries [*know what a congeries is? An arrangement of —a circular arrangement of separate things*] of iridescent globes, the noxious Yog-Sothoth, who froths as primal slime in nuclear chaos forever beyond the nethermost outposts of space and time!

Okay, I'm a kid—you know—I still love that. These things breaking apart and coming together, coming across time and space from another dimension. This is at the end of a story where somebody has unlocked these keys and guards which block these things from coming back, and they're beginning to flow through the opening. He sees them as these separate things which join together and become tentacles. Okay, enough of him.

Michael McClure, in his long poem *Rare Angel,* has these lines completely out of context. But hear how I hear them, given my interest:

> and study the positioning
> of garnets
> on the boulder

Louis Zukofsky, who I'll be talking about more, quoting from Spinoza:

> The more an image is associated with many other things, the more often it flourishes . . . the more causes there are by which it can be excited.

And Thoreau, writing in his Journals:

> Perhaps I can never find so good a setting for my thoughts as I shall thus have taken them out of. The crystal never sparkles more brightly than in the cavern.

James Joyce, in a letter:

> The elements needed will fuse only after a prolonged existence together.

I've had that experience myself, and I think many or all writers have. Write a work and you work on it a long time and it seems to be finished, but there's something wrong. You like it well enough so you don't throw it away, and months later you read it and it's all there. It's right, it's congealed, it's a whole. All those diverse elements have come together correctly. In other words, they give *you* something to think about.

Edgar Allan Poe, from *The Fall of the House of Usher:*

> The conditions of the sentience [*I think that's the correct word, though in my edition it said "sentence," which is somehow more appropriate*] had been here, he imagined, fulfilled in the method of collocation of these stones [*he's talking about the house, which is about to fall*]—in the order of their arrangement, as well as in that of the many fungi which overspread them, and of the decayed trees which stood around—above all, in the long undisturbed endurance of this arrangement, and in its reduplication in the still waters of the tarn.

And Samuel Beckett said:

> It's perhaps all a question of hitting on the right aggregate.

Incidentally, I forgot that I meant to preface this whole talk with two quotes. Samuel Beckett was interviewed, believe it or not, in 1961. I don't know if you know much about him, but he's an extremely private man. He wouldn't be doing *this*. Never. He lives in a very unlisted condition somewhere outside of Paris. But some graduate student from Columbia or New York University tracked him down and grabbed him in a cafe and shoved a tape recorder in front of him, and got him for a minute and he asked him, "Well, what does the artist do now? What's the next thing?" And Beckett said, "To find a form that accommodates the mess, that is the task of the artist now." The mess. The *mess*. And we're in a mess now. Look at—we're packed in here, for one thing. I mean, we have fifteen kinds of electric toothbrushes. TV versions of things. I'd like to say that, in conjunction with my saying that, maybe things are going to go by a little fast and that there may be a *lot* of things in this, that's what you have to deal with. Somehow you have to do that. You have to pick up on it, use it, avoid it, do something with it.

And the other quote to book end this whole thing was from Morton Feldman, who's a composer who was a part of John Cage's group, a friend and influence and influenced by and so on. Feldman said, "What was great about the fifties. . . ." And the fifties is a period when I feel I began to wake up about art. I'm a product of the fifties. Larry Fagin, who's a little older, and I have had a lot of talks about this particularly. What were the conditions of the fifties, as opposed to the sixties when there was a tremendous change. I mean the mess really got going in the sixties. That's where the mess took wing, it seems to me. In the fifties if you were "out of it" in high school, you went and got a Dave Brubeck record or something and you took it home and it was *yours* and you listened to it. Maybe you knew one person you could talk to about it. You *discovered* it. You actually discovered it and made it part of you. "What was great about the fifties is that for one brief moment—maybe, say, six weeks—nobody understood art." *Nobody*. That's why it all happened. I mean, he's talking about the abstract expressionists and John Cage and the whole . . . "Because for a short while, these people were left alone. Six weeks is all it takes to get started."

I've talked to Philip Guston about this very thing, and he was there and he was part of that, and he says that the issue in the forties was not "what *kind* of art to make." I mean, these guys had seen Cubism and Surrealism and Chirico and Picasso and the Social Realists in this country in the thirties. It wasn't like which one to choose or how to make something out of that. It was whether you could paint *at all*. Whether art was possible at all. Start from scratch. No kidding. I mean, up against it. So, those two quotes. This is why I like to book end this with them. Because one of them, the Beckett, is a "mess." It's everything, it's "let's have everything," it's "let's grab part of everything." The other one is "nothing." Ignorance. Nobody understood art. What do you do? Okay, those guys started to put paint on again. Make a mark on the canvas and see what that did to the space and see what would come next. In fact, one of the things Guston likes to talk about most is cave art: the first painters, who are incredible if you look at their work. I'm not sure that anyone is more sophisticated. The mark, the first mark. Of course Guston talks about it like Mallarme's statement, "being a civilized first man." In other words, you're in the cave and you've got your stick, but you know all about art, you've been to the Louvre. You're both of those. That's the way he thinks of his condition as an artist now, and it has to do with the Mess. We know everything. I mean, not always "know" in the sense of "understand" everything, but we're exposed to too much of everything.

I also want to say that there are no rules. At least not at first there aren't. If you start with rules, you've really got a tough road. What I think is that you start with materials. You start with matter, not with rules. The rules appear, the limitations appear, and those are *your* limitations and the limitations of the material. Stone has a certain cleavage. You can't make it look a certain way if the stone is not constructed to allow you to do that.

So. Gertrude Stein. I remember my father bringing home a book, when I was about ten or twelve years old, from the library: *Blood On The Dining Room Floor.* I don't know if anyone knows it, but it was like a murder mystery in a way. I looked at it and it was full of these sing-songy, simple, repetitive-but-not-quite things. And I didn't know who the hell she was but I guess my father told me that this was an adult book and was for real people. And he said, look at this thing. So when I did get to read Stein I already knew; there she was. This is part of her *Stanzas In Meditation:*

> Next to next to and does. [*"Next to next to," get that. "Next to" and "next to," two states. And "does": active, period.*]
> Does it join. [*"Join." Next. . . .*]
> Does it mean does it join.
> Does it mean does it mean does it join. [*Hear those as separate things: "Does it mean does it mean?" She's talking about that too. She's talking about what she just wrote. And "does it join?" And then she says. . .*]
> If after all they know
> that I say so.

It's broken after the "know." "If after all they know *that* I say so," if you want. The hinge is between those two. Okay, join. Things in arrangement join. And let's see what time it is, speaking of arrangements.

I wanted to end up this part of my presentation with a very dangerous thing to do, for me. I'm going to try to talk about a whole poem. To explicate a poem seems to me to be nearly impossible, but I've seen it done once by John Ashbery in an incredible way. I'll tell you about it, but I don't presume to be able to do it. We'll see. He was on a panel discussion at Columbia in the mid-sixties and they had mimeographed copies of his poem *Landscape,* which is in *The Tennis Court Oath* and has incredible lines in it like "the bartender examined the lumps" and "the ladder failed" and things like that. And somebody said—everybody in the audience had a mimeographed copy of this—"Well, what does this mean?" So he took each line and he erected another line from it. In talking about it he created in the air a parallel poem, which was just as fantastic—in my memory of it at least, of the time—as the original poem. But it was a different poem, and he was giving people an example of the artist making up the work right there. I still can't believe it. But he did it, I'm here to tell you.

Now I will proceed not to do that. No chalk. I wish I could play the piano for you. [*writes on blackboard:*]

ounce code orange
a
        the
                      ohm
trilobite trilobites

This is a poem from a group of poems I wrote in 1966, when I was living in Cambridge in the same house with Aram Saroyan, and he was writing these one-word poems, dividing everything down to the smallest possible thing, as I was talking about, and I immediately wanted to put them together. I couldn't stand the idea of one word. I don't think there *is* one word. So this is one of those poems. I did maybe twenty or thirty of these. I suppose they're about as unadulterated, pure, if you will, as anything I ever did. I was really trying to work with the words, look at the words, try to use all their qualities. There's no question of meaning, in the sense of explaining and understanding this poem. Hopefully, it's a unique object, not just an object. Language isn't just objects, it moves. I'll try to talk about some of the qualities of these words that I was aware of when I was writing it, as best I can. It was eleven years ago.

"ounce code orange": ways of measuring, in a sense. Weight, a symbol system, a color. "a/the": the indefinite article, the definite article. "ohm" is the unit of electrical resistance, a quality of metal, let's say, that requires a certain amount of juice to go through. In other words, this is a fuzzy, resistant word. It hangs down here, it affects particularly this space. I wanted these things hanging in the middle because they could adhere to words in either the top line or the bottom line. "*the* ounce," "*a/the* code," "*the* orange." You can't say "a ounce" or "a orange," practically. You can say "a code." So there are those vectors going there. "trilobites": you know what a trilobite is, it's an early animal of the Paleozoic Age that was a crustacean divided into three lobes. As a word, to me it's completely irreducible. What are you going to do with it? "A trilobite": it's like a clinker. Angular, uneven, heavy word. So, I made a plural, and I also say, "trilobite trilobites." That second trilobite becomes a verb. And I feel, as Fenollosa pointed out, that every noun is a verb, and vice versa, and there really are a hell of a lot of them in the English language which don't connect except in being the same word, like the word "saw." "I saw the saw." What sense does that make? Wonderful to work with, though. I also found out later that "ounce" is the name for a kind of leopard. I don't know if anybody knows that. I think it's Indian, or Tibetan. It's a cat called an ounce. So, you think of "pounce." There are these words that begin to adhere and appear like ghosts around these things. Ounce, pounce, bounce. "code"—I don't know, that's beginning to seem a little neutral to me. "Orange": the color *and* the round thing, the fruit. Now that I've said that, the word "ounce" begins to seem round to me. "A trilobite," "*the* trilobites." That's how that goes. And this is the dead spot of the poem, the resistance: "ohm." And it's also almost like the "Om," the balance.

ALLEN GINSBERG: What was the "ounce code orange" there?

CLARK COOLIDGE: What *was* it? It's like "Ice Station Zebra": "Ounce Code Orange." This just came to me. "Secret

Agent X-1." "Ounce Code Orange." *Code* Orange, the Second World War.

A.G.: An "ounce"?

C.C.: An "ounce code," a weight. I don't want it to be "pounds and ounces." I want it to be some other connection.

A.G.: When did you write that poem?

C.C.: 1966. I can only think of about twenty of those that interested me, that really did interest me. You really can't stay there, and I feel that language moves a great deal more than that.

QUESTION: Did you have any reason for writing it or did the words just come out?

C.C.: I had a reason for getting to the place where I started to write that kind of thing, which I was trying to explain in being influenced by Saroyan putting his one word. He put so much pressure on one word, is what it was. He insisted that that word was the poem. You could talk about art being insistent emphasis. The words really came to me very strongly, as strong things. And I began to think: but I want to put them *together* with that kind of intensity. I want to see what happens. Also, another thing I was interested in, at the time, was making a poem of words that *don't* go together in some ways, that have a resistance, that they *don't go*. That kind of energy. As that word "ohm" has to do, in a way, with electrical resistance.

LARRY FAGIN: In fact, the one-word poems have all the pressure because of the lack of relationship with anything else, any other words, or the relationship with no words being there, which created that pressure that's like a vacuum on the one word. If Aram took the word "ounce" and just put it there, all the pressure would be on the "ounce," and this is exactly the opposite, which is about the pressure between the elements. If you had only one element . . .

C.C.: I want these things to affect each other.

L.F.: That's a different kind of arrangement.

C.C.: Yeah. His poems seemed to be under a bell jar with all the air removed.

Q: Did you pick "ounce" because that was a particularly small unit?

C.C.: No. Just the word; the sound and whatever ramifications of meaning it had at that time, which as I say, I can't really recreate now, entirely. I have to think them *again.* This is what you have to do with old poems, you have to see them again.

A.G.: A two-part question. What were you doing just before and what did you move to after? And was there any influence from Ashbery's *Europe* at that time?

C.C.: The year before these poems, I was very influenced by Ashbery's *The Tennis Court Oath,* which came out in the early sixties. *Europe* was absolutely the poem that turned me on and mystified me. I found out later what he did. He took a book called *Beryl of the Byplane* that he found in Paris and used that for phrases right out of the book, so there was a sort of narrative ghost to that poem inside the structure. I didn't see that at all. All I saw were these constellations of words. In fact, some of them really are just that. Does anyone have the book? Here, section twenty-six is simply: "water," way over here. Next line "thinking," and under "thinking," "a," the small letter "a." I thought, wow, he's doing something with almost nothing! A fantastic opportunity to try. Not that it's easier. It *isn't* easier. I don't even know what that poem I wrote [*on the blackboard*] is, frankly, now. It's too late. I put it up there because it mixes in with the talk about arrangement. You can see clearly the separations of those words and that is an arrangement. That's why I put it up, not to justify that as a poem. It was part of my process at the time. I'm glad Allen asked me what I did after this. Before this, I wrote a lot of poems made somewhat like the other poems in this book [The Tennis Court Oath].

A.G.: What's the structure or arrangement of those? I'm not familiar with this field of poetry.

C.C.: Somewhat surrealist. Using American—I always think of Ashbery as a *suburban* American—tone and diction, which I could identify with closely. I always thought he was influenced by painting, although Ashbery himself said that he really wasn't. So that's either him denying what's true, or I'm wrong. Of course Ashbery did spend a lot of time writing art criticism around the time of this. I believe these poems were written in Paris when he was writing daily reviews of art shows. What he says about it is that it was the discipline of having to write on something at the typewriter every day that most influenced him, not the fact that it was on paintings. I can't believe this. I mean, look at these.

Q: I can see the logic in your poem. You can start out with "trilobite trilobites" and think of "trilobite" used as a verb like "fossil," then picture the fossil of a trilobite to be like the sections of an orange, flattened out, threaded. Then, if you use your "ohm" as in fabrics of electricity, all right? And then you picture an orange opening up into packets like ounces, and also words. The words "orange" and "ounce": the e-endings, the o's, and the configurations and symbols of the words, the actual hieroglyphic symbols and iconography of the words. And then I picture this impact of webs and laces of particles. You know how an orange section has many little sections like a trilobite? So it has logic.

C.C.: Sure, yeah, I'm glad you see the interlacing. Next?

Q: You've sort of explained the arrangement and graphed out how the words are inter-reacting together and how they stand alone. While you were writing it, was there any preconceived idea of what you were going to do or was it completely spontaneous?

C.C.: I didn't know what words were going to come. I remember that I wrote that quite quickly except that there were some other words later, which I erased, that I realized were not part of this constellation. I felt myself about to use the word "energy." Anyway, I erased those words and it was quick. The whole time it takes to talk about it here is so much longer than the time it took to do it.

L.F.: Would you cast this poem in terms of bebop?

C.C.: No. It's not a bebop poem. There's no way this has the. . .

A.G.: Is that an abstract expressionist poem?

C.C.: Sure. It was influenced by some of those guys. Guston and DeKooning and. . .

A.G.: In terms of placing one brush stroke after another, it seems like pasting words up in a way.

C.C.: In a way, except that I typed them right out. I didn't use any cut-up, although I had done cut-ups before this. From reading Burroughs in 1963, 1964.

L.F.: What about finding pockets of this kind of thing in people like Whalen's poetry? I mean, literal little constellations within poetry which have a syntax that's recognizable.

C.C.: I'm bound to leave out fifteen or twenty people who had an effect on these kinds of things. These poems, as I feel now, form a pocket in my own poetry. They're very strange, because I have a feeling that language inevitably moves and changes, probably from the influence of being a musician. That seems like a very sad thing now. I can't even read it. Visually, I thought I had a thing to talk about.

Q: When you were studying geology, did you study any higher mathematics like non-linear algebra and trigonometry?

C.C.: No. I was terrible in mathematics in high school.

Q: That seems to me to be a crazy matrix that has no equation kind of meaning like "put it together like a sentence and it's going to mean *that.*" It's just like an over-all abstract message, like an alchemical key.

C.C.: Yeah, maybe. Except, what's it a key to?

Q: I don't know.

C.C.: An attempt to be a key maybe. No, I have no mathematical competence whatsoever.

Q: Have you ever made psychological. . . Remember you talked about the vision of what you called an intrauterine type of enveloping? Have you ever linked that with your love of caves?

C.C.: In my high school yearbook, a friend of mine wrote, "to Clark who loves to go in caves" and something about Freud. Well, what can you do with that? I mean, sure, but. . .

Q: But remember that you said at first; that it was a force in another dimension, which I can get to. You said your friend said it was intrauterine, but you said that you felt that it was a force in another dimension.

C.C.: It was stretching. You're talking about the ship?

Q: It was the ship you said you couldn't describe in this dimension.

C.C.: Yeah, because the closest I can come to it is something that's simultaneously a slot in a substance and a wire right out in the middle of space. You know what I mean? It's both things at once, and it pulls and tugs, and it goes this way and you're caught in it. It's horrible, it's a nightmare. This was a recurrent nightmare. So when I was six or seven I'd wake up screaming.

Q: Were you afraid of caves at first?

C.C.: No. I'm more afraid of caves now than I was then, because I haven't done it regularly in a long time and I find that it's a particular activity in using those muscles and your mind in a particular direction. And if you lay off for a while, then you do begin to be afraid, and you do begin to think that all this rock is going to come down on you, which it's not, it's paranoia. You have to keep doing it. It's like playing an instrument. You get rust. Fear is like being rusty.

Q: I can't really see a connection in meanings in the terms, and I think that in that way you succeeded in what you said you were trying to do; break out of a meaning net. But I can see something very much in the sound. For one thing, it sounds like you could almost play this on the drums. And secondly, just about all the words except the two articles ring some change on the sound "o." It's very constant.

C.C.: Yeah. So obvious I didn't even mention it. Well, "trilobite trilobites": it sounds like a rudiment, a paradiddle or something you have to practice. That's what I don't like. It's not [*hums a bop rhythm*]. You know, it's not as shapely, which I've tried to do more of since.

Q: Is there any way of understanding the shape that comes out?

C.C.: You mean the way the words are arranged? Only to

make spaces in which those things in the center can attach to one side or the other. There's no significance to the fact that it looks like a "Z."

Q: You seemed to mention that they were coming out spontaneously and supposedly just random words. How do you know the fact that there is some connection? How does one word somehow reach another?

C.C.: I hope you didn't understand that I mean "random." I *don't* mean "random." I don't think that's possible. They're coming from a place where you are working in your mind. Does anyone know Anton Ehrenzweig's book, *The Hidden Order of Art?* He's got a term that's a ten-dollar word: "dedifferentiation." What it means is that a young child or an artist has a place in their mind where they can hold many many elements, many diverse elements, ready to be put into something they're making. I mean, many more than you're conscious of. I feel that apparatus—I didn't want to call it subconscious, let's make it a little more sharp—I think that goes on, and that there is a selection process. *That,* rather than random. It isn't like "give me another one. I'll use it."

Sources

ASHBERY, JOHN, *The Tennis Court Oath* (Middletown, Conn.: Wesleyan University Press, 1962).

BECKETT, SAMUEL, "Text for Nothing/8," *Stories and Texts for Nothing* (New York: Grove Press, 1967), p. 114.

COOLIDGE, CLARK, *Space* (New York: Harper and Row, 1970), p. 68. Reprinted by kind permission of the author.

DRIVER, TOM, "Beckett by the Madeleine," *Columbia University Forum, IV,* Summer, 1961), p. 23.

EHRENZWEIG, ANTON, *The Hidden Order of Art* (Berkeley and Los Angeles: University of California Press, 1967).

FELDMAN, MORTON, "Give My Regards to Eighth Street," *Art in America,* March-April, 1971, p. 99.

GODARD, JEAN-LUC, "La Chinoise," *Jean-Luc Godard,* ed. Jean Collet, (New York: Crown Publishers, Inc., 1970), p. 145.

GUSTON, PHILIP, "Philip Guston's Object—A Dialogue with Harold Rosenberg," *Philip Guston—Recent Paintings and Drawings* (New York: The Jewish Museum Catalogue, 1965).

HERACLITUS, "Fragment 124," from Robert Smithson, "A Sedimentation of the Mind: Earth Projects," *Art Forum* (Sept., 1968).

JOYCE, JAMES, *Letters* (New York: Viking Press, 1957).

LOVECRAFT, H.P., "The Call of Cthulhu," *The Dunwich Horror and Others* (Sauk City, Wisc.: Arkham House, 1963), pp. 144-145.

——— and Derleth, August, "The Lurker at the Threshold," *The Watchers Out of Time and Others* (Sauk City, Wisc.: Arkham House, 1974), p. 147.

MCCLURE, MICHAEL, *Rare Angel* (Los Angeles: Black Sparrow Press, 1974), p. 33. Reprinted by kind permission of the author.

PADGETT, LEWIS, "Mimsy Were the Borogroves," *A Gnome There Was (And Other Tales of Science Fiction and Fantasy)* (New York: Simon and Schuster, 1950), pp. 169-172.

POE, EDGAR ALLEN, "The Fall of the House of Usher," *The Complete Tales and Poems of Edgar Allen Poe* (New York: Modern Library, Random House, 1967), p. 239.

STEIN, GERTRUDE, "Stanza LX," Reprinted by permission of Yale University Press from *Stanzas in Meditation* by Gertrude Stein, p. 139. Copyright © 1956 by Alice B. Toklas.

THOREAU, HENRI DAVID, *Journals* (New York: Dover Publications, 1962), vol. 3, p. 334.

ZUKOFSKY, LOUIS, *Bottom: On Shakespeare* (Austin, Texas: The Ark Press, University of Texas Press, 1963). Quoting Spinoza, *Ethics,* p. 29.

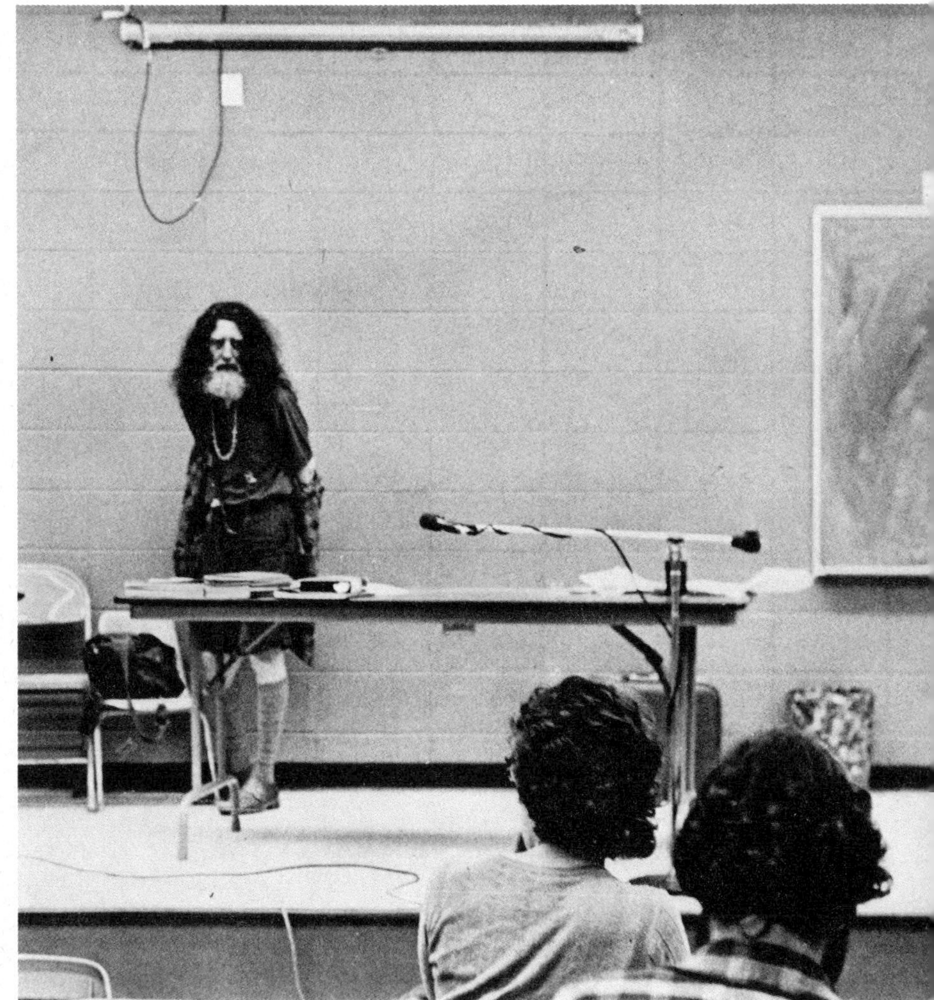

Photo by Rachel Homer

Jackson Mac Low

THE POETICS OF CHANCE AND THE POLITICS OF SIMULTANEOUS SPONTANEITY, OR THE SACRED HEART OF JESUS (REVISED & ABRIDGED)

JULY 12, 1975

In 1954 I began working in a different way than I had previously, under the influence of Taoism & Buddhism, especially Zen Buddhism, together with ideas implicit, some explicit, in the *Book of Changes.* Largely through contact with John Cage's work & friendship, I became interested in using chance operations & similar means, using *words* as he & other composers (Earle Brown, David Tudor, Christian Wolff, & Morton Feldman) were using sounds in the early 50's. This important group of American composers began working together in the later 40's & continued as a group for several years. Some of them, especially Cage, used chance operations, systematically finding ways of getting sound events into compositions & performances without the composer making the choices. One can do this in two different ways, & my program the other night illustrated both. In a minute I'll come to the motives: why a composer or poet wd want to do such a thing. But generally, one uses "objectively hazardous" means—such as random digits, dice, cards, roulette wheels (random-digit tables are really computerized roulette wheels), the methods by which one consults the *Book of Changes,* or methods which look for certain letters at specific places in words—to extract from materials selected in some way or other, or taken from a whole environment of possible materials, various elements to include in an art work.

The dadaists & surrealists called this "objective hazard." I call it "systematic chance" to distinguish it from the kind of chance that's directly related to human impulse, such as that used by Jackson Pollock, the painter. He has often been said to have worked by chance, but his was a highly controlled kind of chance that had a great deal to do with his personality & how he flung things around. He was real careful where he was flinging things even though the exact placement & area of the drip or squiggle of paint was not entirely defined by him consciously. We could call that "impulsive chance." Then there is pure chance, like finding a dime on the street, & that's a beautiful kind which very often adds to everything. Systematic chance is a little more pedantic, but it's a way of working with chance. It's a little different also from what William Burroughs started to do around 1960, when he began to cut up texts & put them together. His so-called "cut-up" method is another form of unsystematic chance, but it's a little more removed from the choice of the author than impulsive chance. The cut-up is in-between objective hazard or systematic chance & impulsive chance.

So the use of systematic chance is one way in which you can avoid making choices, and the reasons for this are involved with the illusoriness of the ego & the wish to dissolve or at least de-emphasize the ego. Another way is for the composer of pieces for groups to make many choices available for performers within the piece. This has been going on for a very long time in music. In the Baroque Era, a great deal of the music was improvised, and the notes that are written down are the notes between which they did very elaborate figuration, as you can read in books such as Arnold Dolmetsch's *The Interpretation of the Music of the XVII & XVIII Centuries*[1], which is mainly a book about ornamentation. There's usually been a great deal of freedom for the individual performer, though probably less in the nineteenth century than before in the history of music. Even then, however, a virtuoso was allowed to let loose in an improvised cadenza toward the end of the Sonata-Allegro movement of a concerto. Such improvisatory freedom has returned to so-called "serious music" recently, since the 50's, and has increased in the 60's and 70's. Composers have been writing pieces that involve a large amount of performer choice, all the way from completely free improvisation to improvisation using given materials following certain procedures, but having many parameters under the control of the individual performer. In such works, there are some elements "that make the piece a piece" & on whose use the composer insists. The performers must work with these elements, but so many of their choices will be individually made that the relation between their egos and the composer's ego provides a situation that goes beyond individual egos. (One must assume good will on the part of everybody participating.)

I composed *5 biblical poems,* my first chance-generated poems, in December 1954 and January 1955. They drew words from the Jewish Publication Society translation of the Jewish Holy Scriptures and were produced by a very simple system using one die, half of a pair of dice, to make poems that look like this:

5.2.3.6.5., THE 3RD BIBLICAL POEM

5.2.3.6.5., THE 3RD BIBLICAL POEM [*1st 2 stanzas*]
sustenance|______|and|______| |______|
|______| |______|
|______| |______|bullock,
of twenty|______| |______| |______|children
hands,|______|came and|______|
|______|weight threescore|______|the
upon|______|
Schechem|______| |______|
|______| |______|he|______|his against
|______| |______|Jephthah, cities|______|

The little boxes indicate silences (each lasting as long as *any* word readers wish to say to themselves). This is a chance-produced structure, each line of which comprises a certain number of events. For at this point I began to work with a new kind of meter, or verse, which I later called "eventual verse," meaning that in place of the foot or syllable or other units used in traditional verse, one uses the "event." In these poems, the event can either be a silence equal to any word readers think to themselves, or a word, a single free form. In making the structures for the *5 biblical poems,* the die determined the number of events per line & the number of lines per stanza, & however many lines are in a stanza, there are that many stanzas, so some of the biblical poems are very long. The last one is very short, it has a three-line stanza, comprising 21, 21, & 29 events in corresponding lines; that's why it's named "21.21.29." This was the first time I wrote anything for simultaneous voices. At that time I called it "the first biblical play," but it's obviously my first "simultaneity." You just *think* a word for each box, make a sound at the end of each line, & make a different sound at the end of each stanza. I prefer a "neutral" delivery rather than one overly expressive or "dramatic." But everything else, such as how fast & how loud you read, how you interpret the words, conversational expressiveness, etc., is up to the performers. They have to follow this particular score & the few rules, including one asking them to make one non-vocal sound at the end of each line & another at the end of each stanza.

Now why do such a thing? From about 1945 I had been involved with Taoism: I considered myself a Taoist. From 1953 on, through contact with friends of Cage, Cage himself, & Dr. D.T. Suzuki, I became interested in Zen Buddhism, & for about 20 years I considered myself a Zen Buddhist. In this context, the idea of trying to produce a kind of art that is not egoic seems very important. That's the main motive for "letting in" other things than oneself, randomizing means or other people or the environment, as when performances include long silences: during silences when you, as a performer, don't do anything for a while, other things that are happening become part of the piece. All of these are ways to let in other forces than oneself. At first one thinks one can avoid the ego, make works that are egoless, by chance. This illusion passes after you work this way a while. You realize that making a chance system is as egoic, in some ways, or even as emotional, as writing a poem spontaneously. But at the same time, you realize there *is* something more than just yourself doing it. & by interacting in that way with chance or the world or the environment or other people, one sees and *produces* possibilities that one's habitual associations—what we usually draw on in the course of spontaneous or intuitive composition—would have precluded, for our so-called intuition or taste is always involved with our biographies & habits, & you know that in Buddhism, the ego includes the Unconscious, in the Freudian sense; all the layers of the mind as dealt with in modern psychology are still within the bounds of the ego, & this includes the deep Unconscious.

Dadaists, including Marcel Duchamp, during World War I, were among the first to use objective hazard (chance methods) seriously. Later, when Cage & his friends began using objective hazard in the 50's, it was largely under the inspiration of Duchamp, who had made sculptures during the 'teens by dropping strings & then cutting the forms they delineated out of wood. (He also composed some chance-generated music.) Duchamp was also the first "conceptual" artist in the present sense, & many of his pieces were the ideas themselves of making such works. There is an element of concept art in my own work, although I'm usually as much or more interested in the actual sounds and sights than in the generative ideas.

Anyway, one realizes that despite the fact that the ego is going to make up these systems & pride itself on becoming "Jackson Mac Low, the great poet who makes up chance systems," nevertheless, there is something or other happening, though now I'm not sure what it is. One element which makes it seem spooky, but isn't all that spooky, is what the *I Ching (Book of Changes)* & Jung talk about: a kind of "acausal connection" (Jung's translator's words) between any two things happening at the same time. I myself think that if there is a connection & it does something, it's *some* kind of cause but it's different from the time-linear cause going from past to future. It's *across* any present, between any two things coexisting. That's why, according to the theory of the *Book of Changes,* if you throw a hexagram, what the sages have said about that hexagram is relevant to your present situation & to the question that you are asking, because all of these things exist in the same time area. & I think that one thing that systematic chance does allow (& also the kind of piece where performers' choices determine many aspects of performance) is for something to happen on that synchronous plane. (For such a situation when things happen at the same time & have a significant connection, Jung invented the term translated as "synchronicity.")

Allowing that to happen in works is important. & this has something to do with what in Zen is called the "No Mind," that layer of mind below the Unconscious, the impulses, the instincts, the Id, the deepest deep layer, which is common to all people: the No Mind (Sunyata viewed as an aspect of mentality). From the No Mind, or from emptiness, everything arises. & if one can step aside a little bit, one can allow it to manifest itself: that is the important discovery made by people who began working with chance operations, such as Duchamp & later Cage, whose stepping aside & his motivation for it were deeply involved with Zen Buddhism (both of us studied with Dr. D. T. Suzuki at Columbia in the 1950's).

Later I will say more about chance *per se,* but I would like to get to the other element, the politics, & also its relation to Dharma.[2] An important element in my life has been pacifist-anarchism. I've been a pacifist since grammar school, though I think I went through a militaristic phase around first grade. I've been a serious pacifist most of my life, & since about '45, I've also identified myself as an anarchist. What I mean by this is that things cd get done better in society without a coercive force pushing everybody around. In every governmentally organized society, there's always either an army or a police force or both somewhere, if only in the background. But I really think that people can freely act together in sane ways, relatively spontaneously, as long as they are *aware,* & I think that this is the political side of Dharma. That is, I think that people—to the degree that they understand the way things go, the nature of the actual going on of our experience, & to the degree that they become aware of other people, their emotions, & so on—will find that every aspect of other people will become more and more available to them in social situations. So it would seem that the politics that would be associated with people in relatively enlightened states would be "anarchist," because they would not need other people to tell them how to direct their spontaneity, how to interact with each other. However, some people will still have to figure out specific things, & some will be ringleaders. There's always a need for ringleaders: that's dangerous. You often need someone to help organize action in individual situations, a temporary leader, but there is a great difference between that & what happens when governments solidify and beget permanent bureaucracies. One part of the alleged need for government arises from the fact that people are going to try to do-in other people if they feel threatened. (The other part is that governments make it possible for ruling classes to rule, exploit, & profit.) Anarchists reject even the "good" motivation for government, the belief that people have to be kept in line & will act well with each other only under the threat of "Well, if I don't act well, I'll go to jail; something will happen to me."

I think it is rather hard to think concretely about anarchist politics. In the 60's, many many people went through semi-anarchic situations in communes & so on, & all of the theories of government were probably born again in people's minds as they went through these experiences, when the communes fell completely to pieces because no one would take responsibility, or some guy took over, or a small clique took over: nearly every possibility worked itself out. I think I still believe that a society may be possible, in which, even though people may have to have temporary leaders for specific purposes, they'll be able to be largely self-governing, individuals & local groups & enterprises taking most of the responsibility for anything that happens in the society, from production to the ordinary course of running a city.

I don't really remember how conscious the connection between this & simultaneous poetry was for me at the beginning, but it certainly became obvious to me in the course of time. I started performing my simultaneities in John Cage's New School classes (1957-60). The first one written was performed even before that, in the Spring of '55. John Cage & myself, with M.C. Richards, the poet and potter, did a private performance of "the 5th biblical poem" (written Jan. 1955) for the composer Henry Cowell, when he came to dinner at the Stony Point farmhouse in which Cage, Richards, David Tudor, & others were living. But after that it wasn't performed publicly until 1961. (I began performing publicly in 1960.) Gradually, while doing public performances in the '60's; I came more & more to realize the degree to which this kind of performance was a model for a free anarchist society.

However, from about 1958 to 1961, I wrote & first performed works utilizing very elaborate chance mechanisms to regulate performances. For instance, performing a simultaneity made from the poems in the book *Stanzas for Iris Lezak*[3] involves three kinds of cards: cards with the separated stanzas of the poems on them, & playing cards & number cards to regulate how fast you speak, how loud you speak, how long you are silent between lines & between stanzas, & when you produce sounds on musical instruments. In August 1960, after I'd written a large number of the poems later published in the book, Al Hansen & Dick Higgins asked me to join them in a concert of new music at The Living Theatre, & I decided to use those poems as texts for a performance work. I developed a performance system not only using the separated stanzas, which are typed on 5″ x 8″ filing cards, but also sounds produced on musical instruments & toys. Playing cards regulated speed & loudness of delivery: a king means one is to read very fast, a small number card, very slow; red suits mean loud, black suits mean soft; pointed suits, being more acute, mean *very* loud or soft; rounded-top suits, being less acute, mean *moderately* loud or soft. Well, even in that situation, where there are a number of guides to follow, one person's "moderately loud" might be another person's "soft." So even in these highly chance-regulated works, there is a good deal of choice for the performers.

In the course of the 60's, the more of these pieces I composed & performed, the more I dropped specific chance regulation & left more & more up to the spontaneous choices of the performers. This was a principle used already by some composers in the Cage group in the early fifties, especially Earle Brown, who no longer works with chance. He made graphic scores, beginning, I think in 1953, that are to be interpreted by the performer spontaneously at the instrument during performance. I've heard that he was somewhat annoyed when David Tudor worked out realizations beforehand, rather than doing so during performance. La Monte Young, several other friends, & I performed some of Earle's pieces in this spontaneous way in 1960-61 at The Living Theatre. Then during the 60's and 70's I produced many works in which performers spontaneously choose materials from an array of them & decide how to use them during performances within the limits set by the piece's specific rules, & by the two general rules for all my simultaneities: "Listen!" & "Relate!"

I want to talk a little bit more about the politics. You see, in the situation of performing a work where the composer-poet says, for instance, "Here's a drawing made up of a vocabulary of 960 words. You have the option of choosing any word on the drawing, but once you have chosen a word, you have to do one of two things: either say it, or play or sing it as a series of notes." (One plays or sings the words by translating their letters into pitches.) Those are all of the instructions that you are given except the system of translating the letters of words into pitches. But I emphasize, in fact, I am going to read, the following paragraph from the instructions for performing *A Vocabulary for Peter Innisfree Moore,* 1975, [*see pp. 182-183*] because I think this gets to the heart of the political situation:

"General Considerations ('style,' attitude, etc.,) : Since not only choice of words from the Vocabulary–& thus, for musicians of 'tone' sequences–but also all parameters except the words ([& their corresponding tone] sequences), once they have been chosen, are at the discretion of the performer, great care, tact, courtesy, attention, & concentration, must be given to making every detail of one's performance contribute (as far as one can tell) toward a total sound sequence (including ambient, audience sounds, & outer-environmental sounds [as well as what the other performers are doing]) which the performer wd *choose* to *hear.*"[4]

I ask people to make choices in this situation, that they add to it, at any particular point, something that they wd *choose* to *hear*. Obviously, this involves preferences, quite the opposite of chance operations, where your preferences are put aside, where if a word you don't "want" at all comes up while writing a poem, it goes in anyway. But in this case, I ask each person to add to the situation, or not to add, what they want & how they want, but not to go ego-tripping without regard to what else is happening, which is the worst of wrong notes in performing any simultaneity of mine. But every kind of virtuosity is strongly encouraged, when used with as much consciousness as possible of its place in the total sound, especially its relation to the contributions of the other performers: one must be both inventive and sensitive to others at all times, & not only to other performers but to the total situation. I think this exemplifies both an enlightened & an anarchistic society.

The performance text is analogous to a *given situation,* for instance, that people must build a bridge to cross a certain river. In an anarchist society one would find whoever in the community is best at building bridges & planning structures—civil engineers & so on—& certain of them would take over specific aspects of the given task. In performing a simultaneity, the *given task,* the analogue of the *building* of the bridge is that you are to make some kind of performance out of the materials & rules. Once you have decided to do this, you are asked to be as human & aware as possible, & to embody this awareness in speech & musical sounds, & also to be as good as possible at doing this, especially, to use all your powers, not simply to be a neutral cog in something—not a robot: as Chögyam Trungpa said last night, you don't want uniformity of robots, you want real people making real spontaneous choices—but they have this *situation* to deal with. I mean, you don't just say anything: you have to say (or play) the given words. (Some people can make sentences out of the words, though I rarely do so, except when I'm alone making other poems from these Vocabularies. I find it hard to think of sentences in the midst of performances, but some friends of mine are crackerjack at this, & they reel off sentences; others prefer just playing with the individual words or groups of them.)

I'd like to ask now whether there are any questions? I've talked about the poetics of chance and its relation to Dharma and the politics of spontaneous—relatively spontaneous—simultaneity (or rather simultaneous spontaneity) & its relation to anarchism and Dharma.

QUESTION: The difference between individual ego-tripping & virtuosity is very confusing.

JACKSON MAC LOW: No, a virtuoso is a person who has a great deal of skill & can do many hard things on an instrument or with their voice. They can use this skill in a very egoic way just to show off, to cut the other performers, as they say in jazz, or they can simply be making use of this virtuosity to add all those goodies to the situation. A person who really knows how to play the piano beautifully can play a piece such as this much better than one who plays as badly as I do these days, for instance. Virtuosity means real skill. Not just show-offness. I understand your objection to virtuosity because it tends to lead to show-off music & the like.

But I think one can use virtuosity to transcend showing off, & I think this occurs in our best jazz performances. (My simultaneities & jazz have many things in common, but certain attitude differences are important.)

Q: I am getting the feeling that this is a game that is played. Is that right?

J.M.L.: Well, it's a game to be played—everything is a game to be played—yeah. I don't have any objection to thinking of it in that way: there are certainly ground rules. But it's a game that's noncompetitive. I guess that's what's different from most of the games that we have now: that these games I call pieces are noncompetitive.

I might as well explain the "Vocabularies" now, since I've been using this one as an illustration. In 1968, a conceptual sculptor, painter, & friend of mine named Carl Fernbach-Flarsheim, who was then mounting a language-art exhibit at the Tyler School of Art at Temple University in Philadelphia, wanted me to contribute something to it. So, because he has this incredible name, I decided to make a drawing composed of words spellable with the letters of his name, repeating letters in any single word only as many times as those letters are repeated in the name. I drew this first "Vocabulary" on a paper lithograph plate, & printed many copies from that. I exhibited the plate & gave away the copies, on the backs of which were directions for people to perform a simultaneity in the gallery, using the Vocabulary as text, when they got the copies. (Eventually the plates got lost—when they were sent to an exhibit in Buenos Aires, they were stolen—but I still have some prints from them.) After that I didn't make any Vocabularies for a few years, & I don't think I performed this one. Then in 1972, the poet Daniela Gioseffi sent me a chain letter for visual poets, which asked me to make a visual poem & send it to the Seattle artist Michael Wiater, who edits the magazine *Toothpick, Lisbon, and the Orcas Islands.* So I made "A Vocabulary for Michael Wiater," using letters from his name to spell words on an ordinary piece of typing paper.

A little later I made the first big 14″ x 22″ Vocabulary,

"A Vocabulary for Sharon Belle Mattlin," from that poet's full name. This one was drawn for Sharon's 21st birthday in June 1973. Then in January 1974, when Charlie Morrow invited me to do a concert with his band, I decided to make this Vocabulary for Sharon into a piece that involved instrumental music, by using the German pitch-name system for playing some of the letters. The German pitch names include A, B, C, D, E, F, G, H, & S: B is B flat, H is B natural, and S is E flat. Thus you have, in Sharon's name, five playable letters: S (E flat), H (B natural), A (A natural), B (B flat), & E (E natural). Very few of the words are spelled only with the playable letters, but you skip the other letters. Thus if you choose the word "share," you play only the S, H, A, & E, skipping the R [*plays E flat, B natural, A natural, & E natural on piano*].

In the first performance, with Charlie Morrow's band, we used quite a few instruments. A number of poets such as Armand Schwerner, who is a bass clarinetist, doubled as instrumentalists. We did a number of performances in New York & Syracuse, among them, two with Merce Cunningham & his dancers. & at The Poetry Project at St. Mark's Church in New York in fall 1974, we did a performance with people stationed all around the balcony, half of them speaking & singing or playing from Sharon's vocabulary, half from Vera Lachmann's vocabulary. Those on one side played from Sharon's; those on the other, from Vera's.

I wanted a polychoral effect, as at St. Mark's in Venice, where a wonderful group of composers (Adrian Willaert, Andrea & Giovanni Gabrieli, etc.) invented polychoral music. They influenced Monteverdi, Heinrich Schutz, & eventually J. S. Bach. In that huge cathedral in Venice they had two organs, one at each end, & they could place a chorus near each organ & other choruses elsewhere, the choruses cd answer each other back & forth. I'll do the St. Mark's, Venice, piece yet. The attempt at St. Mark's, New York, didn't work very well. The sounds tended to homogenize because there wasn't enough separation: you couldn't tell who was working from one Vocabulary & who was working from the other, so you didn't get a polychoral effect. You got a sort of all-over stereophonic effect, which was nice, . . . but not polychoralism.

When we performed with Merce Cunningham, we also performed another piece, called *The Black Tarantula Crossword Gathas,* from graph-paper scores similar to the earlier Gathas [*see below*], based on mantra (s), but made up of English words from a book by Kathy Acker. I needed slides of these Gathas, & Peter Moore, who is a great photographer, made me free slides (he wouldn't let me pay him), so I decided to make a Vocabulary from his name, & when I got to talk to him about it, I found that his middle name is Innisfree, which clinched it. His full name includes five E's & three R's, so its letters gave me a list of 960 words. In drawing the previous Vocabularies, I had just entered the words spontaneously as I thought of them, & eventually, when there was no more room, I'd quit. In making Peter's Vocabulary, I made the list first & then drew words from it by using chance operations involving random digits from the RAND Corporation's table *A Million Random Digits with 100,000 Normal Deviates* (The Free Press, Glencoe, Ill., 1955) to draw words, one at a time, from the list; to select which of ten sectors into which the paper was divided should be the one where I would draw a particular word; & to determine in which direction each word's letters would run (there are ten possible directions). The size of the letters & the pen nib used to draw each word were left to my spontaneous choice. I tended to use larger letters & thicker nibs for the words first drawn from the list, which is why some unusual words, such as "mestee," are drawn large and thick and some common words, such as "inn," "its," & "reporters," are drawn small and thin. However, I soon realized that the only German pitch names in Peter's name were E, F, & S, which would be played as the tones E natural, F natural, & E flat, all within a major or minor second of each other. So I decided to make a system in which I translated *all* the letters into tones: the letter I is played as C sharp; M, B natural; N, C natural; O, F sharp or G flat; P, B natural; R,

A flat or G sharp; S, E flat or D sharp; & D as D natural. [*Plays examples.*] When performing this piece, there are various distinct things that one has to do: for instance, once you have started playing tones corresponding to a particular word, you must play the whole word.

Now I want to tell you about my Gathas. In January 1961, I thought of a type of visual poem & sound-text piece that I call a "Gatha." I used that term because most of the earlier Gathas, those made before 1973, were derived from Buddhist mantra (s), and the term "gatha" is used for the little poems that Zen Buddhist masters & their students used to write to embody their insights. The method I usually use employs chance operations to place the letters of transliterations of a mantram vertically so that they cross an "axis" of A's, U's, & M's placed horizontally in a row of squares on a piece of quadrille graph paper. I use random digits to determine the placement of this "AUM axis" on the paper as well as the number of A's, U's, & M's in the axis. Then other chance operations are used to determine which A, U, or M of the mantram is to coincide with one of the A's, U's, or M's of the AUM-axis. In the case of Gathas derived from mantra (s) which have no U in them at all, such as the Great Prajñāpāramitā Mantram ("GATE, GATE, PARAGATE, PARASAMGATE, BODHI, SWAHA!"), there is a long skinny row of U's in the center of the AUM-axis with empty squares above and below it and columns on either side of it in which the mantram crosses A's and M's in the AUM-axis.

Recently I've been drawing Gathas on black-lined graph paper sent home to me by Mr. Unger, my son's 7th-8th grade math teacher. This is one of them, derived from the most widely used of all the mantra (s), that of the Bodhisattva Avalokiteshvara or Chenrezi, "AUM MANI PADME HUM," which is pronounced "OHM MAHNEE PAYMAY HOONG." He's the All-Seeing-One, the All-Compassionate-One. Psychologically, he can be thought of as the compassion in each of us. Now, there are three A's in this transliteration of the mantram. Since one of these three A's must coincide with each of the A's in the AUM-axis, I used a die to determine which one would do so in each case (a 1 or a 4 wd determine that the A of "AUM" would coincide with an A on the axis; a 2 or 5, the A of "MANI"; a 3 or 6, the A of "PADME"). I did the same with the other letters—that is, I used a die, but threw for "odd" or "even" to determine which of the two U's would coincide with each of the U's on the axis, & I threw for "odd" or "even" twice to determine which of the four M's would coincide with an M on the axis.

But once, by these various chance means, one has placed repetitions of a mantram across an axis of A's, U's, & M's, one can use the resulting configuration in a way quite different from that in which it was produced. Though generated largely by objective systematic chance, it can be used in spontaneous performances. I ask the performers simply to "move" from any square to any other square that is adjacent to one of its sides or corners (that is, they can move in any direction, horizontal, vertical, or diagonal). Thus each performer follows a path on the plane of the quadrille paper. They can say letter names, such as "M"; letter sounds, such as "mmmmmmm"; syllables formed by letters adjacent in any direction (s); words, pseudowords, or word strings formed by letters adjacent in any direction (s); or they can say the whole mantram (they can do that at *any* time, no matter where they are on their path, & can then start a new path at any square on the paper). By each person's producing all of these possibilities at different times in their performance, & by listening very hard to what everybody is doing (as well as to any other sounds that are audible where they're performing), any number of people can perform one of these. Last night, Sharon and I performed a Gatha at the beginning of the program as a duo. At the end, twelve or fourteen people performed a Gatha based on "OM TARE TUTTARE TURE SWAHA," the mantram of Tara, the mother of the Bodhisattvas.

A great deal is thus left up to performers' choices—not only whether to produce letter sounds, letter names, syllables, words, or whole repetitions of the mantram, but *how* to produce or treat these sounds. People are encouraged to sing, & to prolong vowels & liquids. Spontaneous harmonies happen that way: when one person starts prolonging a sound, other people prolong theirs. It comes in waves. In some performances, if you have a lot of real "singy" people, you get one continual organ point evolving into another. But you also get percussive effects by using the dentals and plosives & such [*makes sounds*], and you can get all kinds of rhythms. The performers can do anything they want in the way of rhythms. However, they are not encouraged to make melodies (although they aren't forbidden) just to produce long tones and to speak & to do rhythmic things. [*Mac Low then played tapes recorded at a public concert the previous night of a duo vocal performance with Sharon Mattlin of "Mani Gatha," a 14-voice performance of "Tara Gatha," and part of a performance by voices and instruments of* A Vocabulary for Peter Innisfree Moore.)

Those are pretty good examples of relatively spontaneous simultaneity, or more properly, simultaneous spontaneity. You can hear from these how virtuosity can be nonegoic: someone playing the recorder very well or singing very well can obviously make the piece sound more interesting in some ways, without making ego-expression the end of the performance. In other ways, of course, it's interesting to have untutored sounds, too, & one gets plenty of those. Personally, however, I have been getting more & more choiceful: I like it when the music sounds "nice."

I mentioned earlier the book, *Stanzas for Iris Lezak,* which consists of all the poems I wrote between May and late October in 1960. Since I didn't read any of them at last night's performance, I'd like to do so now, to show a kind of systematic chance-operation poetry that is almost entirely due to things outside of myself. The first "Stanzas" were six poems written for my wife, Iris Lezak. In writing them I devised the system used in the later ones.

Everybody knows what an acrostic is? You know, *B*y *E*ddie *D*uchamps, would be an acrostic for "bed": the initial letters are B, E, D. By spelling words out acrostically with words found in a text, but not knowing what specific words you are going to get, you have a way of producing a poem with many features outside of your control. In writing the first ones, I spelled out: "My girl's the greatest fuck in town. I love to fuck my girl." I spelled this out with single words, one word for each letter, so that each word formed a line, & the space between the two sentences became a silence break, using words from the Bengali poet Rabindranath Tagore's *Gitanjali* (Song Offerings, 1928). I brought into the poem, successively, each word I came to that began with the proper letter, for instance, "my" is spelled with M and Y. "My you" were the first words starting with these letters that came up. I made six poems, each spelling these two particular sentences out. I called this group "Six Gitanjali for Iris." These words were drawn from Tagore's book simply because they were the next words on the page beginning with the proper letters. I don't know whether I got to the pages by numbers. I think I used a number system in these, not in the others, to get me part of the way. [*Reads I, II, & VI.*][5]

6 GITANJALI FOR IRIS

I

My you
Gain is rainy life
See
The Here end
Gain rainy end again the end see the
Feet. Utter. Cry know
Is Now,
The outside when Now,

(18 seconds of silence)

Is
Life outside void end
The outside
Feet. Utter. Cry know
My you
Gain is rainy life

II

Midnight, your
Gifts is river, light,
Sing
Thy humble every
Gifts river, every and thy every sing thy
Flute unbreakable captive keep
Is not
Thy of whom not

(10 seconds of silence)

VI

Morning You
Gleam in resonant life
Shame
Thee. He eyes
Gleam resonant eyes and thee. Eyes shame thee.
From up come Kindle
In not
Thee. Of wall not

(15 seconds of silence)

In
Life of vain eyes
Thee. Of
From up come Kindle
Morning You
Gleam in resonant life

OK, so that was where the system came from. From there on, I just took words, phrases, or sentences from whatever I happened to be reading. Among the things that I had around was a circular that advertised soybeans, entitled, "There are many ways to use Strayer's vegetable soybeans." I used this as I used the sentences that I mentioned before, as the index to draw words out. Perhaps you noticed that words repeated. In one kind of stanza, every time the same letter came up in whatever was being spelled out, the same word or word string was used within a stanza. You notice that "end" came up a number of times in the 1st poem every time "E" appeared in the index sentences. Not all of these are that way. Other stanzas have different words or phrases within stanzas for the same letter, & later on, the units got to be not only words, but word strings, whole sentences, etc. Thus a number of different kinds of linguistic units became the events that fill the places & correspond to the letters of the title.

That's chance. I don't know what word is going to come up next. The rule in the repeating stanza is that every time a letter is repeated in the title, or whatever is used as the index to draw words from a source, that word is repeated in the stanza, but I don't know *what* that word is going to be before I start doing it. & *where* it's going to repeat. I've never figured it out ahead of time. So in that sense, it's a matter of chance.

Notes

1. Dolmetsch, Arnold, *The Interpretation of the Music of the XVII & XVIII Centuries* (London: Novello & Co., Ltd. and Oxford University Press, 1916, 1946).
2. Dharma: truth or what is. In Buddhism, the study of things as they are.
3. Mac Low, Jackson, *Stanzas for Iris Lezak* (Barton, Vt: Something Else Press, 1971-72). Reprinted by permission of the author.
4. ———, *A Vocabulary for Peter Innisfree Moore* (published by the author). Copyright © Jackson Mac Low. Reprinted by permission of the author.
5. ———, "Six Gitanjali for Iris," *Stanzas for Iris Lezak*, op. cit., pp. 203-208.

John Cage

EMPTY WORDS WITH RELEVANT MATERIAL

THIS IS A manuscript and selection of commentary by John Cage on his text *Empty Words. Lecture IV,* the last part of this work, was performed for the first time at Naropa Institute in the summer of 1974.

The first part of this collection is four prefaces written by Cage for the Four Lectures, I-IV. The second part is a note explaining how to read the manuscript pages which follow. These are the first six pages of *Lecture IV*. The final section is a conversation with audience—Naropa students, local and other—after the *Empty Words IV* performance, a most volatile occasion, taking place the same night Nixon resigned.

Editors' Note

FIRST PREFACE

Wendell Berry: passages outloud from Thoreau's Journal (Port Royal, Kentucky, 1967). Realized I was starved for Thoreau (just as in '54 when I moved from New York City to Stony Point I had realized I was starved for nature: took to walking in the woods). Agreed to write work for voices (Song Books [Solos for Voice 3-92]). Had written five words: "We connect Satie with Thoreau." Each solo belongs to one of four categories: 1) song; 2) song using electronics; 3) theatre; 4) theatre using electronics. Each is relevant or irrelevant to the subject, "We connect Satie with Thoreau." Syntax: arrangement of the army (Norman Brown). Language free of syntax: demilitarization of language. James Joyce = new words; old syntax. Ancient Chinese? Full words: words free of specific function. Noun is verbs is adjective, adverb. What can be done with the English language? Use it as material. Material of five kinds: letters, syllables, words, phrases, sentences. A text for a song can be a vocalise: just letters. Can be just syllables, just words; just a string of phrases; sentences. Or combinations of letters and syllables (for example), letters and words, et cetera. There are 25 possible combinations. Relate 64 *(I Ching)* to 25. 64 = any number larger or smaller than 64. 1 — 32 = 1; 33 — 64 = 2. 210 = 46 groups of 3 + 18 groups of 4. Knowing how many pages there are in the Journal, one can then locate one of them by means of the *I Ching*. Given a page one can count the lines, locate a single line, count the letters, syllables (e.g.), locate one of either. Using index, count all references to sounds or silence in the Journal. Or all references to the telegraph harp. (Mureau uses all twenty-five possibilities.) Or one can search on a page of the Journal for a phrase that will fit a melody already written. "Buzzing strings. Will be. The telegraph harp. Wind is from the north, the telegraph does not sound. Aeolian. Orpheus alive. It is the poetry of the railroad. By one named Electricity." ". . . to fill a bed out of a hat. In the forest on the meadow button bushes flock of shore larks Persian city spring advances. All parts of nature belong to one head, the curls the earth the water." "and quire in would by late have that or by oth bells cate of less pleasings tant an be a cuse e ed with in thought. al la said tell bits ev man . . ." "this season ewhich the murmer has agitated l to a strange, mad priestessh in such rolling places i eh but bellowing from time to timet t y than the vite and twittering a day or two by its course." (Was asked to write about electronic music. Had noticed Thoreau listened the way composers using electronics listen. "SparrowsitA grosbeak betrays itself by that peculiar squeakarieffect of slightest tinkling measures soundness ingpleasa We hear!") Project slides: views of Walden Pond. Needed slides but they were not at hand. Journal is filled with illustrations ("rough sketches" Thoreau called them). Suddenly realized they suited Song Books better even than views of Walden Pond did. Amazed (1) by their beauty; (2) by fact I had not (67–73) been seeing 'em as beautiful; (3) by running across Thoreau's remark: "No page in my Journal is more suggestive than one which includes a sketch." Illustrations out of context. Suggestivity. Through a museum on roller skates. Cloud of Unknowing. Ideograms. Modern art. Thoreau. "Yes and No are lies: the only true answer will serve to set all well afloat." Opening doors so that anything can go through. William McNaughton (Oberlin, Ohio: '73). Weekend course in Chinese language. Empty words. Take one lesson and then take a vacation. Out of your mind, live in the woods. Uncultivated gift.

SECOND PREFACE

Part II: A mix of words, syllables, and letters obtained by subjecting the Journal of Henri David Thoreau to a series of *I Ching* chance operations. Pt. I includes phrases. III omits words. IV omits sentences, phrases, words, and syllables: includes only letters and silences. Categories overlap. E.g., a is a letter, is a syllable, is a word. First questions; What is being done? for how many times? Answers (obtained by using a table relating seven to sixty-four): the fourth of the seven possibilities (words; syllables; letters; words and syllables; words and letters; syllables and letters; words, syllables; letters; (obtained from *I Ching*): fifty-two times. Of the fifty-two, which are words? which are syllables? 1–32 = words; 33 — 64 = syllables. In which volume of the Journal's fourteen is the syllable to be found? In which group of pages? On which page of this group? On which line of this page? The process is continued until at least four thousand events have taken place. Poetry. Include punctuation when it follows what is found. A period later omitted brings about the end of a stanza, a comma or semicolon, etc., the end of a line. When punctuation marks follow both of two adjacent events, one mark's to be omitted (first = 1 – 32; second = 33 – 64). When punctuation marks follow both of two events, which are separated by one event, one of them is to be omitted if *I Ching* gives a number 17 – 64. By two events: 33 – 64. By three events: 48 – 64. Elements separate from one another? or connected? What indentation for this line? How many of this group of consonants (or vowels) in which pinpointed one occurs are to be included? How is this text to be presented? As a mix of handwriting, stamping, typing, printing, letraset? Attracted by this project but decided against embarking on it. Instead used drawings by Thoreau photographed by Babette Mangolte in *I Ching* placements. Ideograms. Of the four columns on two facing pages which two have text? Which drawing goes in this space? Each space now has one. Into which spaces do the remaining drawings go? Where in the spaces? Divide the width and the height into sixty-four parts.

THIRD PREFACE

Searching (outloud) for a way to read. Changing frequency. Going up and then going down; going to extremes. Establish (I, II) stanza's time. That brings about a variety of tempi (short stanzas become slow; long become fast). To bring about quiet of IV (silence) establish no stanza time in III or IV. Not establishing time allows tempo to become naturally constant. At the end of a stanza simply glance at the second hand of a watch. Begin next stanza at next 0 or 30. Instead of going to extremes (as in I and II), movement toward a center (III and IV). A new breath for each new event. Any event that follows a space is a new event. Making music by reading outloud. To read. To breathe. IV: equation between letters and silence. Making language saying nothing at all. What's in mind is to stay up all night reading. Time reading so that at dawn (IV) the sounds outside come in (not as before through closed doors and windows). Half-hour intermissions between any two parts. Something to eat. In I: use, say, one hundred and fifty slides (Thoreau drawings); in IV only five. Other vocal extremes: movement (gradual or sudden) in space; equalization. (Electronics.) Do without whatever's inflexible. Make a separate *I Ching* program for each aspect of a performance. Continue to search.

FOURTH PREFACE

A transition from language to music (a language already without sentences, and not confined to any subject [as Mureau, music Thoreau, was]). Nothing has been worked on: a journal of circa two million words has been used to answer questions. Another reservoir? *Finnegans Wake.* Another? Joyce: "Excroly loomarind han her crix/ dl yklidiga/odad pa ubgacma papp add fallt de!/ thur aght uonnon." Languages becoming musics, musics becoming theatres; performances; metamorphoses (stills from what are actually movies). At first face to face; finally sitting with one's back to the audience (sitting with the audience), everyone facing the same vision. Sideways, sideways.

NOTES ON THE MANUSCRIPT

Included here are the first sixteen pages of *Lecture IV,* [*pp. 201-216*] the fourth part of *Empty Words.* The third part ends at the top of the first page. These parts are just a sample of the text. "L" means letter; "LS" means letters or silences. "S" means silence. 64 (the number the *I Ching* works with) was related to 16, so that the first four silences (14″, 2″, 16″ and 9″) resulted from numbers between 57 and 60, between 5 and 8, between 61 and 64, and between 33 and 36. The entire text has 4018 events. These six pages have 280 events. The Roman numbers refer to the volumes of Thoreau's *Journal* (I-XIV). The numbers which follow them refer to the page in the volume. Since each volume began with page three, it was necessary to write the number given by the *I Ching* (two chance operations: one for a group of pages, the second for the particular page in that group) and follow it with the third page from it (counting it) . I then found the line on the page, counted the letters in the line, and found with the *I Ching* which letter was to be notated. If I received a vowel in a group of vowels, or a consonant in a group of consonants, I asked how many were to be used and which, including of course the first one received. The notated liaisons are for performance. That is, the fifth and sixth events, "i" and "e" are to be pronounced sequentially in one breath, followed by "th" and "a" in one breath. The twelfth, thirteenth, and fourteenth events are not pronounced "bath," but "B" plus "a" plus "th" in one breath. The numbers in circles (e.g. "twenty-five at the beginning") give the number of events which are "L" or "S" or "LS" as the case may be. The numbers in circles accompanied by " are time notations. Where periods followed letters received through chance operations, the ends of "Paragraphs" were given. The underlined letters, such as *u* (event 257) were italics in the original and therefore, in performance, are to be vocalized spontaneously.

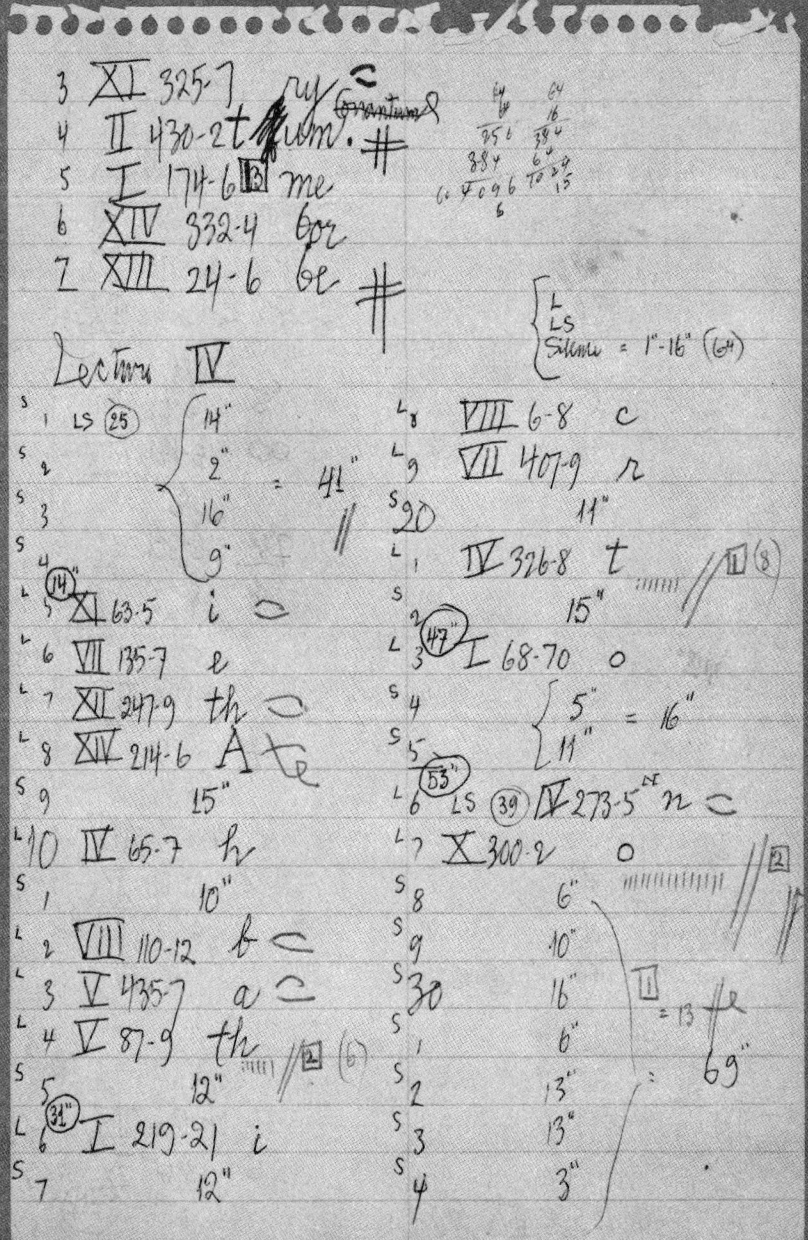

3 XI 325-7 ry
4 II 430-2t
5 I 174-6 [3] me
6 XIV 332-4 bpr
7 XIII 24-6 be

L
LS
Silence = 1"-16" (64)

Lecture IV

S 1 LS (25) 14"
S 2 2"
S 3 16" = 41"
S 4 9"
L 5 (14") XI 63-5 i
L 6 VII 135-7 e
L 7 XII 247-9 th
L 8 XIV 214-6 A te
S 9 15"
L 10 IV 65-7 h
S 1 10"
L 2 VIII 110-12 b
L 3 V 435-7 a
L 4 V 87-9 th [2] (6)
S 5 12"
L 6 (31") I 219-21 i
S 7 12"

L 8 VIII 6-8 c
L 9 VII 407-9 r
S 20 11"
L 1 IV 326-8 t [II] (8)
S 2 15"
L 3 (47") I 68-70 o
S 4 5"
S 5 11" = 16"
L 6 (53") LS (39) IV 273-5 r
L 7 X 300-2 o [2]
S 8 6"
S 9 10"
S 30 16"
S 1 6"
S 2 13"
S 3 13"
S 4 3"
[II] = 13 = 69"

S	5 (1'17")		2"	
L	6	XI 219-21	s	
L	7	XIII 132-4	n	
S	8		16"	=26"
S	9		10"	
L	40	I 418-20 [1]	i	
S	1		5"	
L	2 (1'30")	XIV 119-21	e ⊂	
L	3	XIV 274-6	r	
S	4		13"	
L	5 (1'35")	X 14-16	t	
L	6	XII 253-5	s	
S	7		6"	
L	8 (1'38")	I 186-8	p	
L	9	IX 125-7	rt	
S	50		3"	
L	1	XIV 131-3	oo	
L	2	IV 87-9	s,	
S	3 [2]		11"	
L	4 (1'47")	XI 322-4	sp ⊂	
L	5	VII 445-7	wl ⊂	
L	6	IV 189-91	a ⊂	
L	7	V 19-21	e	
S	8		8"	16"
S	9		8"	

L	60	VII 335-7 str	(1'55")
S	1	4	= 20"
S	2	5	
S	3	6	
S	4	5	
	5 S (58)	12	
	6	12	
	7	15	
	8	9	
	9	6	
	70	16	
	1	12	
	2	15	= 187"
	3	15	
	4	5	
	5	8	
	6	11	
	7	4	
	8	1	
	9	11	
	80	15	
	1	5	
	2	4	
	3	12	
	4	9	

5	14"
6	7
7	6
8	6
9	7
90	14
1	4
2	8
3	14
4	15
5	11
6	2
7	8
8	4
9	5
100	2
1	8
2	3
3	11
4	16
5	3
6	10
7	1
8	12

191"

9		12"
110		12"
1		3"
2		15"
3		13"
4		15"
5		5"
6		8"
7		6"
8		6"
9		5"
120		9"
1		14"
2		7"
S 3	SL (58)	4"
S 4		13
S 5		14
L 6	(5'06") 220-2	0
S 7		6"
S 8		7"
S 9		6"
S 130		6"
S 1		8"
L 2	(5'19") 151-3"	V

187
191
130"

= 508
= 6'28"

= 31" [2]

= 33" [3]

S 3 2" } = 11"
S 4 (5'23") 9"
L 5 XIV 32-4 n ⊂
L 6 VIII 337-9 n
L 7 I 154-6 psymp ⊂
L 8 VIII 394-6 nts, ⊂
L 9 VIII 101-3 r ⊂
L 140 XIII 167-9 e, ||
S 1 IX e 3" } = 8"
S 2 5"
(5'33")
L 3 III 263-5 d. S
L 4 XIII 74-6 o
L 5 X 262-4 t ⊂
L 6 VII 243-5 st
S 7 10"
(5'45")
L 8 VI 112-4 h
L 9 V 467-9 r
S 150 7" } = 9" |||
S 1 2"
L 2 XI 447-9 i
(5'45")
L 3 IV 25-7 h
S 4 7" } = 8"
S 5 1"
L 6 XIII 2-4 u ⊂(V)
L 7 VIII 76-8 ou

L 8 VII 11-13 i
S 9 V 7"
L 160 VII 73-5 e
L 1 III 454-6 n ⊂
L 2 V 483-5 nb
S 3 8" } |||| 33"
S 4 11"
S 5 1"
S 6 (6'06") 13"
L 7 X 135-7 t
S 8 11" } 31"
S 9 4"
S 170 16" ||||
(6'17")
L 1 XI 403-5 tyw
S 2 10"
L 3 IV 209-11 t
S 4 2"
L 5 II 333-5 e
S 6 9" } 35"
S 7 4"
S 8 9"
S 9 13"
(6'35")
L 180 XIV 325-7 n
1 S (32) 16" } || 29"
2 13"

3 1
4 16
5 5
6 13
7 8
8 9
9 6
190 11
1 13
2 15
3 1
4 4 183"
5 4
6 9
7 14
8 5
9 4
200 1
1 12
2 4
3 8
4 4
5 12
6 14

7 13 = (4'22")
8 2
9 3 50"
210 4 183 =
1 14 29
2 14 808" = 262
3 L 55 VI 174-6 y
4 V 452-4 rr 810"
5 III 396-8 rt
6 X 181-3 fgr
7 II 124-6 l
8 IV 475-7 g
9 IV 429-31 ndw (w)
220 IX 383-5 f
1 XI 391-3 t
2 XIV 228-30 g
3 I 150-2 g
4 VI 320-2 c
5 V 181-3 w
6 X 359-61 e
7 VI 487-9 a
8 IX 11-3 t
9 III 129-31 e
230 X 59-61 i

1 XII 371-3 n
2 IX 191-3 i ‖II
3 VI 120-2 c ⌒
4 III 4-6 b ⌒
5 X 221-3 ll ⌒
6 V 225-7 t ⌒
7 VII 97-9 i
8 II 351-3 o
9 X 109-11 o (825")
840 XIII 336-8 z
1 II 86-8 eo ⌒
2 VI 344-6 th ⌒
3 V 68-70 e
4 VIII 378-80 a ⌒
5 XIII 59-61 pl
6 V 83-5 mb ⌒
7 XI 312-4 eae
8 II 361-3 r
9 IX 221-3 tytr ⌒
850 III 404-6 hm
1 IX 287-9 o ‖II
2 V 100-2 a ⌒
3 XIII 42-4 rh
4 XI 368-70 rt
5 IX 166-8 f ⌒

6 IV 474-6 ththth (840")
7 IV 251-3 u ⌒
8 XI 51-3 tsδ ⌒
9 VII 360-2 δtw
260 VIII 138-40 r ⌒
1 VIII 402-4 e ⌒
2 XII 73-5 e ⌒
3 VIII 134-6 e
4 IX 45-7 a
5 VI 297-9 a ⌒
6 VI 482-4 a
7 VI 206-8 gh ‖II
8 s (56) 9"
9 7"
270 11"
1 4"
2 7"
3 9"
4 10"
5 13"
6 2"
7 1"
8 9"
9 5"
280 2"

= 89" ‖

1	6"		5	11	
2	9"		6	8	
3	16"		7	3	
4	10		8	2	
5	2		9	15	
6	8		310	5	
7	5		1	11	
8	1		2	16	
9	9		3	7	89
290	14		4	5	177
1	15	17 7"	5	1	153"
2	3		6	13	
3	7		7	5	= 419
4	4		8	14	
5	2		9	12	= 6'59"
6	15		320	10	
7	11		1	11	
8	4		2	2	
9	2		3	2	
300	7		S 4 LS (33)	4	: 15"
1	1		S 5	11 (11'13")	
2	7		L 6 XI	128:30	
3	6		S 7	9" (11'18")	
4	13		L 8 XIII	161-3	u (U)

L 9	XII	275-7	e	
L 330	III	20-2	s	⌢
L 1	II	28-30	ea	
S 2		13"		
L 3	V	171-3	e	⌢
L 4	X	394-6	a	
L 5	XIII	118-20	e	⌢
L 6	VI	460-2	rr	
L 7	XIV	322-4	i	
L 8	XI	255-7	ea	
S 9	X	12"	|||||	[6] |||||
L 340	III	235-7 (11'33")	o	
S 1		4"		
L 2	I	204-6"	l	
S 3		7" } = 12"		
S 4		5"		
L 5	XIII	75-7	b	⌢
L 6	III	266-8	rs	
L 7	XV	26-8	s,	||
L 8	XI	368-70 (11'46") [2]	sth	
S 9		10" } 14"		
S 350		4"		
L 1	VIII	405-7"	r	⌢
L 2	XIII	383-5	i	
S 3		10"		

L 4	VIII	328-30	i	
L 5	IV	195-7	w	
S 6		3" } = 9"		||
S 7	LS (63)	6"		
L 8	XI	234-6 (12'01") [2]	ly	
S 9		6"		
L 360	III	279-81	i	⌢
L 1	VII	323-5	e	⌢
L 2	IX	276-8	nl	
S 3		14"		
S 4		10" } = 48" [2]	|||||	||
S 5		14"		
S 6		10"		
L 7	XIII	194-6 (12'22")	a	
S 8		10"		
L 9	IV	237-9	l	
L 370	X	391-3	i	
L 1	III	101-3	sg	||
L 2	VII	427-9 [1] (12'31")	o	
S 3	✝	1"		
L 4	VII	493-5	ll	
S 5		2"		
L 6	IV	68-70	nc	
S 7		40"		
L 8	VII	260-2	δ	⌢

L 9 II 151-3 lkw
S 380 11"
S 1 13" } = 26" |||||
S 2 2" (12'48")
L 3 II 499-501 a
L 4 XI 374-6 oo
S 5 4 } = 7"
S 6 3
L 7 I 349-51 t
S 8 16" } = 18"
S 9 2"
L 390 XI 33-5 u (U)
L 1 IV 367-9 e
L 2 I 434-6 u (U) (13'01")
S 3 13" (13'05")
L 4 XIII 188-90 o
S 5 13
S 6 2 } = 20"
S 7 5
L 8 XIV 153-5 ou
S 9 1"
400 VI 125-7 s,
L 1 III 453-5 [19] c (13'22")
L 2 II 319-21 t.

(14'01") [2]
L 3 XIV 170-2 t
L 4 XI 332-4 l
L 5 III 272-4 m
L 6 XIV 87-9 rdt
S 7 4" } = 11"
S 8 7"
L 9 IX 121-3 e
L 410 XI 425-7 t
L 1 XI 26-8 sh
L 2 XIV 165-7 gg [2]
S 3 15" (14'16")
L 4 XIII 283-5 δ
S 5 16"
L 6 XIII 251-3 a
L 7 XIV 229-31 n
S 8 14" } = 22" [2]
S 9 8"
420 S (42) 7
1 1
2 6
3 3 } = 46"
4 16 [2]
5 9
6 4

7	15	
8	16	
9	6	
430	2	
1	4	
2	6	
3	9	
4	9	
5	5	
6	14	
7	16	
8	6	
9	16	= 208
440	16	
1	1	
2	5	
3	7	
4	5	
5	6	
6	4	
7	7	
8	1	
9	13	
450	4	
1	15.	

	2			11		
	3			3		
	4			6		
	5			7		46
	6			13		208
	7			4		= 88"
	8			13		
	9			10		= 342
	460			8		= 5'42"
	1			13		
S	2	LS (57)		15"	(16'31")	
L	3	XIV	320-2	a		
L	4	IX	317-9	e		
S	5			15	= 28"	
S	6			13	(16'42")	
L	7	XIV	68-70	io		
L	8	IX	250-2	t		
S	9			3"		
L	470	XIII	329-31	ou		
L	1	IX	18-20	u		
L	2	X	251-3	ou.		
L	3	V	469-71 (17'21")	rtl		
L	4	V	87-9	th		
S	5			6"		
L	6	X	488-90	e		

S 7 8 } = 21"
S 8 13
L 9 I 135-7 th
S 480 13"
L 1 III 249-51 io (17'38")
S 2 12"
L 3 V 501-3 e
L 4 IX 423-5 f
L 5 IX 367-9 P.M.-T
L 6 IX 451-3 a
L 7 XIV 6-8 n
S 8 6"
L 9 XIV 215-7 r [2]
L 490 IV 23-5 (17'51") a
L 1 VII 458-60 thpr
S 2 4
S 3 13
S 4 6 = 42"
S 5 6
S 6 13 [2]
L 7 XI 343-5 (18'08") tly
S 8 10
S 9 9 = 20"
S 500 1

L 1 XI 302-4 K
L 2 XII 403-5 a
L 3 V 162-4 e
L 4 XII 400-2 s
L 5 II 279-81 i
S 6 5" [2] (18'21")
L 7 VII 57-9 fr
S 8 6"
L 9 VIII 254-6 ea
L 510 IX 248-50 a
S 1 12"
L 2 XIII 24-6 r
L 3 VI 205-7 i
S 4 8 } = 22"
S 5 14 [2] (18'38")
L 6 X 7-9 nt
S 7 9"
L 8 XII 73-5 br
9 L (27) IX 131-3 n
520 VIII 7-9 s
1 XII 384-6 ea
2 VII 215-7 ∞
3 I 424-6 th
4 VII 275-7 h

5 (18'58")	IX 252-4 [10]	n ⊂
6	VI 484-6	i ⊂
7	VII 460-2	rn ⊂
8	XI 4-6	i ⊂
9	II 482-4	δth
530	VIII 445-7	l .
1	XI 33-5	δ
2	VI 120-2	ngstr ⊂
3	VIII 379-81	a
4	XI 299-307	r
5	V 457-9	t ⊂
6	VII 321-3	l
7	VI 471-3	i ⊂
8	XIV 29-31	a ⊂
9	VII 436-8	e ⊂
540	IX 168-70	a
1	II 101-3	y
2	IX 156-8	w ||
3	XIV 185-7 [24]	i (19'14")
4	XIV 160-2	h
5	I 424-6	ea ⊂
6 L (28)	I 327-9	o
7	X 257-9	i ⊂
8	XIV 20-2	tp. #
9 (19'49")	XII 251-3 [11]	ee ⊂

550	X 365-7	ea ⊂
1	XI 189-91	e ⊂
2	IX 498-500	h
3	IV 10-12	g ⊂
4	I 93-5	ei ⊂
5	XIV 174-6	e ⊂
6	VI 190-2	r ⊂
7	X 118-20	rδs
8	XI 450-2	s ⊂
9	IX 1-3	n
560	XIII 283-5	i ⊂
1	V 165-7	e ⊂
2	XIII 28-30	nδt ⊂
3	XI 422-4	ngh ⊂
4	II 170-2	tc-h
5	I 288-90	t, [6] th ⊂
6	IV 372-4	⊂
7	V 129-31	e ⊂
8	VII 88-90	s ⊂
9	VI 469-71	ft
570	V 219-21	t ⊂
1	IV 214-6	ng
2	XIII 413-5	w
3	IX 255-7	oo ⊂
4 L S (35)	VII 5-7	ɛ: ||

(20'19") [3]

L 5 VIII 319-21 w ⊂

L 6 VIII 263-5 r

S 7 11 }

S 8 3 } = 14"

L 9 VIII 34-6 w (N)

S 580 14 }

S 1 1 } 21"

S 2 6 } //

L 3 II 201-3 [2] rdst

L 4 III 164-6 (20'34") r

S 5 13 }

S 6 11 } = 24"

L 7 X 45-7 o

S 8 9" //

L 9 VIII 466-8 [2] yr

S 590 11"

L 1 IX 75-7 (20'51") tr ⊂

L 2 XII 277-9 t

L 3 I 481-3 fy

L 4 II 86-8 s

S 5 16"

L 6 II 206-8 s

S 7 8 }

S 8 12 } 20" ||| // [2]

S 9 9 }

S 600 10 } 25

S 1 3 } 20

S 2 3 } 45"

// [1]

L 3 I 42-4 o ⊂

L 4 IX 204-6 t

L 5 II 338-40 (21'19") δ ⊂

L 6 IV 230-2 ou ⊂

L 7 XIII 155-7 dh ⊂

L 8 II 223-5 √

9 S (23) 7

610 2

1 6

2 14

3 2 // [1]

4 11

5 5 123

6 9

7 3

8 8 [2]

9 14 // |||||||

620 16

1 15 [2]

2 11 ||| //

3	16	8	3
4	9	9	16
5	14	650	4
6	4	1	1
7	10	2	3
8	13	3	11
9	13	4	10
630	2	5	2
1	1	6	3
2 5	4	7	1
3	13	8	2
4	1	9	2
5	1	660	16
6	12	1	8
7	12	2	12
8	16	3	15
9	6	4	5
640	2	5	14
1	10	6	15
2	11	7	15
3	13	8	8
4	16	9	4
5	5	670	16
6	12	1	12
7	2	2	13

3 9
4 7
5 3 [1]
6 2' || 136
7 11 211
8 12
9 15 = 122
680 10 ||| [1] 469
1 5
2 15 = 7'49"
3 9
4 12 |||||| [1]
5 12 (24'47")
6 L (19) VI 437-9 e
7 IV 53-5 I ⌒
8 V 145-7 ts
9 IV 86-8 n; th ⌒
690 XII 419-21 ly, r
1 IX 327-9 O
2 II 361-6 rn
3 VI 332-4 i ||
4 XI 435-7 [24] h
5 XI 42-4 o ⌒
6 X 365-7 rly

7 III 86-8 h ⌒
8 V 342-4 s ⌒
9 XIV 17-9 (25'08") l
700 VIII 267-9 n
1 VII 222-4 gr ⌒
2 IV 42-4 n. # (25'43")
3 VIII 119-21 [2] b
4 V 20-2 th
L 5 LS (7) VI 266-8 a
S 6 2"
L 7 II 1-3 e
S 8 12"
L 9 VII 476-8 s. M
L 710 XIV 131-3 pl
S 1 6" } = 12" ||
S 2 LS (34) 6"
L 3 XIV 197-9 [8] (25'58") u (U)
S 4 9" } = 25"
S 5 16"
L 6 VIII 3-5 CK; th || [1] (26'13")
S 7 11"
L 8 XII 262-4 n
L 9 I 438-40 r
S 720 2"

L 1	I 163-5	s	6	s (58)	5
L 2	XIII 280-2	chh	7		6
S 3	11		8		6
S 4	1		9		6
S 5	16	= 44	750		13
S 6	6		1		12
S 7	6		2		8
S 8	4	(26'33")	3		10
L 9	XII 18-20	t	4		14
S 730	11		5		11
S 1	2	= 19"	6		15
S 2	6		7		13
L 3	I 325-7	m	8		12
S 4	11		9		14
S 5	13		760		10
S 6	10	= 40"	1		16
S 7	4		2		10
S 8	2	(26'55")	3		11
L 9	XIII 66-8	yh	4		1
L 740	VII 74-6	m	5		4
L 1	X 426-8	o	6		1
S 2	11		7		13
S 3	3	(27'00)	8		12
L 4	VIII 213-5	t	9		10
L 5	XIII 2-4	бw (W)	770		16

249

EMPTY WORDS IV

Empty Words IV took place August 8, 1974. Slide projections of drawings from Thoreau's *Journal* slowly appeared and disappeared as John Cage, sitting at a table, back to the audience, his text lit by a small lamp, performed the sounds of vowels, consonants and silences of his piece. Some of the audience filled in the silences with sounds ranging from guitar playing and bird whistles, to catcalls and screams. Through it all Cage managed a fierce concentration on his piece. When it was over he rose and turned to face the audience. The following dialogue ensued:

QUESTION: You've said that the key of sound is that all sounds pertain to nature. And that you are trying to portray that.

JOHN CAGE: I didn't say that at all. I didn't say I was trying to portray anything—and if you had listened closely you would have understood that.

Q: In light of what happened, do you think you were sucking people out of themselves?

J.C: There was no sucking going on. [*Uproar*]. I think we all, I too, not only you, have a good deal of self-examination to do. I can tell you a story—it happened years ago, and it has happened throughout my life. This isn't the first time people have tried to make me appear as a fool. I went with Merce Cunningham to Columbus, Ohio, in the forties. We drove night and day through snow and ice, often slipping off the road, to get to Columbus. We arrived so late that there was no time to sleep. We had to prepare in the theatre, and then gave the performance. There was a party afterwards. And at the party everyone told us how miserable our work was, and why did we devote our lives to what we were doing? And I thought at the time, why do we go to such trouble to do these things that people don't enjoy?

Ten years later I received a letter from a person who had been at that particular program, and he thanked me for that performance, and said that it had changed his life. Now whether his life changed for the better we don't know—but at least it gave him some kind of stimulus.

Q: Did you enjoy the noises?

J.C: I was doing something I had never done before. And the reason that I decided to do it here was that it occurred to me that it was very beautiful and very appropriate for this circumstance. But then due to my becoming so foolishly famous, many people come to such a performance who have no reason for coming except a foolish curiosity. And when they discover that I'm not nearly so interesting to them as they thought I might be, I don't understand why they don't go away.

Q: Isn't that the chance response you deal with?

J.C.: I know it, I know what limb I'm out on. I've known it all my life, you don't have to tell me that.

Q: It's just like those slides you showed, the response was just a different thing.

J.C: Nonsense. Those slides are by Thoreau and in my opinion they are extremely beautiful. The catcalls and imitations were mere stupid criticisms. The thing that is beautiful about the Thoreau drawings is that they're completely lacking in self-expression. And the thing that made a large part of the public's interruption this evening so ugly was that it was full of self-expression.

Q: Why draw a line?

J.C: It's the line that I've drawn, and to which my life is devoted. I had the good fortune in the late forties to go for two years to lectures by Daisetz Suzuki on Zen Buddhism. One of the lectures he gave was on the structure of mind. He drew an oval on the board, and halfway up the left-hand side he put two parallel lines which he said was the ego. "The ego has the capability to close itself in by means of its likes and dislikes. It stays there by day through its sense perceptions and by night through its dreams. What Zen would like, instead of its acting as a barrier, is that the ego would open its doors, and not be controlled by its likes and dislikes."

Q: I want to know how you organized the silent spaces.

J.C: When you're dealing, as I was this evening, with just letters and silences, there are three possibilities: one is to have a series of letters, another is to have a series of letters and silences, and the last is to have a series of silences. The *I Ching* works with the number 64. I have made tables for the numbers up to 64. The question is which of the three possibilities are we doing? I assigned to letters alone 1 through 21; 22 through 43 the two together; and 44 through 64 the silences. The whole text this evening began with fourteen seconds of silence, followed by a mixture of letters and silences. I find the letters by asking which of the fourteen volumes I am looking in; which group of pages; which page. Then I count the lines on the page, and then count the letters in the line and find one of the letters. And if there were vowels together, or two or more consonants together, I asked the *I Ching* whether I should take one or more of the consonants or vowels, because in that way one gets diphthongs or other sounds that separate us from the simplicity of the alphabet.

Q: I think the work was a success, I think you really got your point across.

J.C: No, I didn't get my point across to you, you got your point across to you. I don't know why you still think people are pushing ideas from one head into another.

Q: Did you end the piece the way you wanted to end it, or did you end it because people were making noise?

J.C: I didn't end it the way I wanted to end it, I ended it the way it was to end. Why is it that when I go to hear someone and I don't like what is going on, instead of interrupting it, I say to myself, why don't you like it? Can't you find something about it that you enjoy? People insist upon self-expression. I really am opposed to it. I don't think people should express themselves in that kind of way.

Q: But isn't that what you're doing right now?

J.C: I don't think so, I'm discussing this situation, which although you say you enjoyed it, I think could have been a lot more successful.

Q: Haven't you said that you want to incorporate outside noises into your work?

J.C: I haven't said that, I've said that contemporary music should be open to the sounds outside it. I just said that the sounds of the traffic entered very beautifully, but the self-expressive sounds of people making foolishness and stupidity and catcalls were not beautiful, and they aren't beautiful in other circumstances either.

Q: But are they a part of the work?

J.C: No. They're a part of the experience we have. They are a part of our lives, but are they a part of what we want society to be?

Q: It's what we are.

J.C: No—I think society can be different.

Q: Yes, but it's what we can start with, work with.

J.C: I must say that since '67 I've worked on the journals of Thoreau. Thoreau said that when he was in the presence of nature, he had a feeling of affirmation about life. He said when he was with people he couldn't find it. I think that answer is easily found without it being told by anyone.

Q: What were your expectations of your performance tonight?

J.C.: I don't have expectations.

Q: If you're disappointed, then you have expectations.

J.C: That goes back to what I said at the beginning, that I felt that it would be beautiful to do this piece in this situation.

Q: Aren't you glad you got an honest response?

J.C: If we are talking about the interruptions, that's not to be classified under honest, that's to be classified under the complete absence of self-control and openness to boredom—and boredom comes not from without but from within.

Sources

THOREAU, HENRI DAVID, *Journals,* 14 vols. (New York: Dover Publications, 1962).